HARRAP'S

Italian

PHRASE BOOK

Compiled by
LEXUS

with

Maria Luisa Lee

PARRAGON

First published in Great Britain 1988
by HARRAP BOOKS Ltd

© *Chambers Harrap Publishers/Lexus Ltd* 1988

This edition published in 1994 by
Parragon Book Service Ltd.
Avonbridge Industrial Estate
Atlantic Road, Avonmouth
Bristol BS11 9QD

Printed in Italy

CONTENTS

INTRODUCTION

The phrase sections in this new book are concise
and to the point. In each section you will find: a
list of basic vocabulary; a selection of useful
phrases; a list of common words and expressions
that you will see on signs and notices. A full
pronunciation guide is given for things you'll want
to say or ask and typical replies to some of your
questions are listed.

Of course, there are bound to be occasions when
you want to know more. So this book allows for
this by containing a two way Italian-English
dictionary with a total of some 5,000 references.
This will enable you to build up your Italian
vocabulary, to make variations on the phrases in
the phrase sections and to recognize more of the
Italian words that you will see or hear when
travelling about.

As well as this we have given a menu reader
covering about 200 dishes and types of food — so
that you will know what you are ordering! And,
as a special feature, there is a section on
colloquial Italian.

Speaking the language can make all the difference
to your trip. So:

buona fortuna!
bwona fortoona
good luck!

and

buon viaggio!
bwon vee-ajo
have a good trip!

PRONUNCIATION

In the phrase sections of this book a pronunciation guide has been given by writing the Italian words as though they were English. So if you read out the pronunciation as English words an Italian person should be able to understand you. Some notes on this:

double consonants (bb, ll, mm etc) have been written 'b-b', 'l-l', 'm-m' etc to remind you that Italians pronounce each of the two consonants, as when you say 'lab building' or 'full list';

letters in bold type in the pronunciation guide mean that this part of the word should be stressed.

hello
buongiorno; (*evening*) buona sera
bwonjorno; bwona sayra

hi
ciao
chow

good morning
buongiorno
bwonjorno

good evening
buona sera
bwona sayra

good night
buonanotte
bwonanot-tay

pleased to meet you
piacere
pee-achayray

goodbye
arrivederci
ar-reevedairchee

cheerio
ciao
chow

see you
arrivederci
ar-reevedairchee

yes
sì
see

GENERAL PHRASES

no
no
no

yes please
sì grazie
see gratsee-ay

no thank you
no grazie
no gratsee-ay

please
per piacere
pair pee-achayray

thank you/ thanks
grazie
gratsee-ay

thanks very much
molte grazie
moltay gratsee-ay

you're welcome
prego
praygo

sorry
mi scusi
mee skoozee

sorry? (*didn't understand*)
come dice?
komay deechay

how are you?
come sta?
komay sta

very well, thank you
benissimo, grazie
baynees-seemo gratsee-ay

and yourself?
e lei?
ay lay

GENERAL PHRASES

excuse me (*to get attention*)
scusi!
skoozee

how much is it?
quanto costa?
kwanto kosta

can I ...?
posso ...?
pos-so

can I have ...?
vorrei ...
vor-ray

I'd like to ...
vorrei ...
vor-ray

where is ...?
dov'è ...?
dovay

it's not ...
non è ...
non ay

is it ...?
è ...?
ay

is there ... here?
c'è ... qui?
chay ... kwee

could you say that again?
potrebbe ripetere?
potrayb-bay reepaytairay

please don't speak so fast
potrebbe parlare più lentamente
potrayb-bay parlaray pyoo lentamentay

I don't understand
non capisco
non kapeesko

GENERAL PHRASES

OK
va bene
va baynay

come on, let's go!
su, andiamo!
soo and-yamo

what's your name?
come si chiama?
komay see k-yama

what's that in Italian?
come si dice in italiano?
komay see deechay een eetal-yano

that's fine!
va bene!
va baynay

aperto	open
chiuso	closed
divieto di . . .	. . . forbidden
donne	ladies
entrata libera	admission free
non . . .	do not . . .
per piacere . . .	please . . .
proibito	forbidden
rifiuti	litter
si prega di . . .	please . . .
signore	ladies
signori	gents
spingere	push
tirare	pull
uomini	gents
vendesi	for sale
vernice fresca	wet paint
vietata l'affissione	stick no bills
vietato	forbidden
vietato l'ingresso	no entry

COMING AND GOING

airport	l'aeroporto	*a-ayroporto*
baggage	il bagaglio	*bagalyo*
book (in advance)	prenotare	*prenotaray*
coach	il pullman	*poolman*
docks	il porto	*porto*
ferry	il traghetto	*traget-to*
gate (at airport)	l'uscita	*oosheeta*
harbour	il porto	*porto*
plane	l'aeroplano	*a-ayroplano*
sleeper	la cuccetta	*koochet-ta*
station	la stazione	*stats-yonay*
taxi	un taxi	*taxee*
terminal	il terminal	*tairmeenal*
train	il treno	*trayno*

a ticket to ...
un biglietto per ...
oon beel-yet-to pair

I'd like to reserve a seat
vorrei prenotare un posto
vor-ray prenotaray oon posto

smoking/ non-smoking please
fumatori/ non fumatori, per piacere
foomatoree/ non foomatoree pair pee-achayray

a window seat please
un posto vicino al finestrino, per piacere
oon posto veecheeno al feenestreeno pair pee-achayray

which platform is it for ...?
da quale binario è in partenza il treno per ...?
da kwalay beenaree-o ay een partentsa eel trayno pair

11

COMING AND GOING

what time is the next flight?
a che ora parte il prossimo volo?
a kay ora partay eel pros-simo volo

is this the right train for ...?
è questo il treno per ...?
ay kwesto eel trayno pair

is this bus going to ...?
questo autobus va a ...?
kwesto owtoboos va a

is this seat free?
è libero questo posto?
ay leebairo kwesto posto

do I have to change (trains)?
devo cambiare (treno)?
dayvo kamb-yaray (trayno)

is this the right stop for ...?
è questa la fermata per ...?
ay kwesta la fairmata pair

which terminal is it for ...?
qual'è il terminal per ...?
kwalay eel tairmeenal pair

is this ticket OK?
va bene questo biglietto?
va baynay kwesto beel-yet-to

I want to change my ticket
vorrei cambiare il biglietto
vor-ray kamb-yaray eel beel-yet-to

thanks for a lovely stay
grazie per la vostra ospitalità
gratsee-ay pair la vostra ospeetaleeta

thanks very much for coming to meet me
grazie per essermi venuto incontro
gratsee-ay pair es-sairmee venooto eenkontro

well, here we are in ...
bene, eccoci a ...
baynay aykochee a

12

niente da dichiarare?
n-yentay da deekya-raray
anything to declare?

le spiace aprire la borsa?
lay spee-achay apreeray la borsa
would you mind opening this bag please?

allacciare le cinture di sicurezza	fasten your seat belts
arrivi	arrivals
bagaglio a mano	hand luggage
biglietti	tickets
binario	platform
coincidenza	connection
controllo passaporti	passport control
dogana	customs
entrata	entrance
fumatori	smoking
imbarco immediato	boarding now
non fumatori	no smoking
partenze	departures
prenotazione obbligatoria	booking essential
ritardo	delay
ritiro bagagli	baggage claim
sala d'attesa	waiting room
stazione ferroviaria	railway station
tenere la destra	keep right
timbrare il biglietto nella macchina	stamp your ticket in the machine
uscita	exit, gate

GETTING A ROOM

balcony	un balcone *balkonay*
bed	un letto *let-to*
breakfast	la prima colazione *preema kolats-yonay*
dinner	la cena *chayna*
dining room	la sala da pranzo *sala da prantso*
double room	una camera doppia *kamaira dop-pya*
guesthouse	la pensione *pens-yonay*
hotel	un albergo *albairgo*
key	la chiave *kee-avay*
lunch	il pranzo *prantso*
night	una notte *not-tay*
private bathroom	un bagno privato *ban-yo preevato*
reception	la reception *'reception'*
room	una camera *kamaira*
shower	una doccia *docha*
single room	una camera singola *kamaira seengola*
with bath	con bagno *kon ban-yo*
youth hostel	un ostello della gioventù *ostel-lo del-la joventoo*

do you have a room for one night?
vorrei una camera per una notte
vor-ray oona kamaira pair oona not-tay

do you have a room for one person?
vorrei una camera per una persona
vor-ray oona kamaira pair oona pairsona

do you have a room for two people?
vorrei una camera per due
vor-ray oona kamaira pair doo-ay

I have a reservation
ho prenotato
o praynotato

GETTING A ROOM

we'd like to rent a room for a week
vorremmo affittare una camera per una settimana
vor-raym-mo af-feet-taray oona kamaira pair oona set-teemana

I'm looking for a good cheap room
vorrei una camera bella e a buon mercato
vor-ray oona kamaira bel-la ay a bwon mairkato

how much is it?
quanto costa la camera?
kwanto kosta la kamaira

can I see the room please?
posso vedere la camera, per piacere?
pos-so vedayray la kamaira pair pee-achayray

does that include breakfast?
la prima colazione è compresa nel prezzo?
la preema kolats-yone ay komprayza nel pretso

a room overlooking the sea
una camera con la vista sul mare
oona kamaira kon la veesta sool maray

we'd like to stay another night
vorremmo restare ancora una notte
vor-raym-mo restare ankora oona not-tay

we will be arriving late
arriveremo la sera tardi
ar-reevairaymo la sayra tardee

can I have my bill please?
potrebbe preparare il mio conto, per piacere?
potrayb-bay prepararay eel meeo konto pair pee-achayray

I'll pay cash
pago in contanti
pago een kontantee

can I pay by credit card?
accettate le carte di credito?
achet-tat-tay lay kartay dee kraydeeto

15

will you give me a call at 6.30 in the morning?
può svegliarmi alle 6.30 domani mattina?
pwo svel-yarmee al-lay say ay metsa domanee mat-teena

at what time do you serve breakfast/ dinner?
a che ora servite la prima colazione/ la cena?
a kay ora sairveetay la preema kolats-yonay/ la chayna

can we have breakfast in our room?
possiamo fare la prima colazione in camera?
pos-syamo faray la preema kolats-yonay een kamaira

thanks for putting us up
grazie dell'ospitalità
gratsee-ay delospeetaleeta

1° piano	first floor
2° piano	second floor
albergo della gioventù	youth hostel
ascensore	lift
bagno	bathroom
camere da affittare	rooms to rent
completo	no vacancies
doccia	shower
mezza pensione	half board
parcheggio riservato ai clienti dell'albergo	car park for hotel residents only
pensione	guesthouse
piano	floor
pianterreno	ground floor
sala da pranzo	dining room
si prega di lasciare libera la camera prima di mezzogiorno	please vacate your room by twelve noon
si prega di non disturbare	please do not disturb
sotterraneo	basement
uscita di sicurezza	fire escape

EATING OUT

bill	il conto *konto*
dessert	il dolce *dolchay*
drink	bere *bayray*
eat	mangiare *manjaray*
food	i cibi *chee-bee*
main course	il secondo piatto *sekondo pee-at-to*
menu	la lista *leesta*
restaurant	il ristorante *reestorantay*
salad	un'insalata *eensalata*
service	il servizio *sairveets-yo*
starter	l'antipasto *anteepasto*
tip	la mancia *mancha*
waiter	il cameriere *kamair-yayray*
waitress	la cameriera *kamair-yayra*

a table for three, please
un tavolo per tre, per piacere
oon tavolo pair tray pair pee-achayray

can I see the menu?
vorrei vedere la lista
vor-ray vedayray la leesta

we'd like to order
vorremmo ordinare
vor-raym-mo ordeenare

what do you recommend?
che cosa consiglia?
kay koza konseel-ya

I'd like ... please
vorrei ... per piacere
vor-ray ... pair pee-achayray

waiter!
cameriere!
kamair-yayray

17

EATING OUT

waitress!
camariera!
kamair-yayra

could we have the bill, please?
il conto, per piacere
eel konto pair pee-achayray

two white coffees please
due caffè con latte, per piacere
doo-ay kaf-fay kon lat-tay pair pee-achayray

that's for me
quello è per me
kwel-lo ay pair may

some more bread please
dell'altro pane, per piacere
del-laltro panay pair pee-achayray

a bottle of red/ white wine please
una bottiglia di vino rosso/ bianco per favore
oona bot-teel-ya dee veeno ros-so/ bee-anko pair favoray

albergo	inn
donne	ladies
menù del giorno	today's set menu
menù fisso a 10.000 lire	set menu costing 10,000 lire
piatti da portar via/ da asportarsi	take-away meals
servizio (non) compreso	service charge (not) included
si prega di ritirare lo scontrino alla cassa	please get your receipt from the cash desk (*without this you won't get served*)
tavola calda	café serving food
trattoria	restaurant
uomini	gents

aceto vinegar
acqua minerale gassata sparkling mineral water
acqua minerale non gassata still mineral water
acqua naturale still mineral water or tap water
aglio garlic
agnello al forno roast lamb
albicocche apricots
ananas pineapple
anatra duck
anguria water melon
antipasti starters
antipasti misti variety of starters
aperitivo aperitif
aragosta lobster
arancia orange
arrosto di tacchino roast turkey
arrosto di vitello roast veal
basilico basil
besciamella white sauce
bistecca (di manzo) beef steak
bistecca ai ferri grilled steak
brasato braised beef with herbs
brioche type of croissant
brodo clear broth
brodo di pollo chicken broth
cannelloni al forno rolls of egg pasta stuffed with
  meat and baked in the oven
capretto al forno roast kid
carciofi artichokes
carciofini sott'olio little artichokes in oil
carote carrots
castagne chestnuts
cavoletti di Bruxelles Brussels sprouts
cavolfiore cauliflower
cavolo cabbage
cetrioli cucumber

MENU READER

cicoria chicory
ciliege cherries
cipolle onions
cocktail di gamberetti prawn cocktail
coniglio arrosto roast rabbit
coniglio in salmì jugged rabbit
consommé consommé (concentrated clear broth)
contorni vegetables
costata alla fiorentina T-bone steak
cotoletta ai ferri grilled veal cutlet
cotoletta alla milanese veal cutlet in breadcrumbs
cotoletta alla valdostana veal cutlet with ham and
  cheese cooked in breadcrumbs
cozze alla marinara mussels in garlic sauce
crema al caffè coffee cream pudding
crema al cioccolato chocolate cream pudding
crema di funghi cream of mushroom soup
crema pasticciera confectioner's cream custard
crocchette di patate potato croquettes
crocchette di riso rice croquettes
crostata di frutta fruit tart
datteri dates
dentice al forno baked type of sea bream
dolci desserts, gateaux etc
fagiano pheasant
fagioli beans
fegatini di pollo chicken livers
fegato liver
fegato alla veneta (cotto al burro con cipolle) liver
  cooked in butter with onions
fettuccine ribbon-shaped pasta
fichi figs
filetto ai ferri grilled fillet of beef
filetto al pepe verde fillet of beef with green
  peppercorns
finocchio fennel
fonduta (al formaggio con latte e uova) cream made
  with cheese, milk and eggs
formaggi misti variety of cheeses
fragole strawberries
frappé ice-cold milk shake

frittata type of omelette
frittata al formaggio cheese omelette
frittata al prosciutto ham omelette
frittata alle verdure vegetable omelette
fritto misto mare mixed seafood in batter
frutta secca dried nuts and raisins
frutti di mare seafood
funghi mushrooms
funghi trifolati mushrooms fried in garlic and parsley
gamberetti prawns
gamberi crayfish
gamberoni king prawns
gelatina gelatine
gelato ice cream
gnocchi little flour and potato dumplings
gnocchi alla romana little milk and semolina
  dumplings baked with butter
grancevola spiny spider crab
granita drink with crushed ice
granita di caffè drink with crushed ice and coffee
grigliata mista mixed grill (meat or fish)
grissini thin, crisp breadsticks
indivia endive
insalata salad
insalata di pesce seafood salad
insalata di riso rice salad
insalata russa Russian salad
insalata verde green salad
lamponi raspberries
lasagne al forno lasagne
lattuga lettuce
legumi vegetables such as beans, peas, lentils etc
lenticchie lentils
lepre hare
limone lemon
lingua tongue
lingua salmistrata pressed tongue
macedonia di frutta fruit salad
maiale pork
mandarino mandarin orange
mandorle almonds

manzo beef
marzapane marzipan
mascarpone very rich clotted cream
mela apple
melanzane aubergines
melone melon
meringhe con panna meringues with fresh cream
merluzzo cod
minestra in brodo noodle soup
mozzarella in carrozza slices of bread and mozzarella
  dipped in egg and fried
nasello hake
nocciole hazelnuts
noci walnuts
nodino (di vitello, con l'osso) veal chop
omelette ai funghi mushroom omelette
omelette al formaggio cheese omelette
orata al forno baked gilthead
ostriche oysters
paglia e fieno mixture of ordinary and green (spinach)
  tagliatelle
paillard di manzo o vitello slices of grilled beef or veal
parmigiana di melanzane layers of aubergines,
  tomato sauce, mozzarella and parmesan, baked
patate potatoes
penne type of pasta quills similar to maccheroni
peperonata peppers cooked in a tomato sauce with
  onions
peperoni peppers
pera pear
pesca peach
pesce fish
pesce al cartoccio fish baked in foil with herbs
pesce in carpione soused fish
pesce persico perch
piselli peas
pizza Margherita pizza with tomato, mozzarella and
  basil
pizza napoletana pizza with tomato, mozzarella and
  anchovies
pizza quattro stagioni pizza with tomato, mozzarella,

    ham, mushrooms and little artichokes
pizzaiola slices of beef cooked in tomato sauce, oregano and anchovies
polenta maize meal boiled in water with salt until firm and cut into slices
pollo chicken
pollo alla cacciatora chicken chasseur (in white wine and mushroom sauce)
pollo alla diavola chicken pieces flattened and deep-fried
pomodori tomatoes
pompelmo grapefruit
porri leeks
prezzemolo parsley
prosciutto ham
prosciutto cotto cooked ham
prosciutto crudo/di Parma dry-cured ham
purè di patate creamed potatoes
radicchio chicory
ragù sauce made with mince, tomatoes and diced vegetables
rapanelli radishes
razza skate
rigatoni ridged pasta tubes
riso rice
risotto rice cooked in clear broth till broth has evaporated
risotto alla milanese (allo zafferano) risotto flavoured with saffron
rosmarino rosemary
salmone affumicato smoked salmon
salsa di pomodoro tomato sauce
salsa verde sauce for meats made with chopped parsley and oil
saltimbocca alla romana slices of veal rolled with ham and sage and fried
salvia sage
scaloppine veal escalopes
sedano di Verona Veronese celeriac
selvaggina game
semifreddo dessert made of ice cream, sponge etc and served cold

senape mustard
sogliola sole
sogliola alla mugnaia sole cooked in flour and butter
spaghetti alla carbonara spaghetti with egg, chopped
  bacon and Parmesan cheese sauce
spaghetti alla matriciana spaghetti with minced pork
  and tomato sauce
spaghetti alle vongole spaghetti with clams
spezzatino di vitello veal stew
spiedini small pieces of different meats or fish cooked
  on the spit
spinaci spinach
stracciatella beaten eggs cooked in boiling, clear broth
stufato meat stew
succo di frutta fruit juice
sugo sauce
svizzera hamburger
tagliatelle al basilico thin, flat strips of egg pasta and
  chopped basil
tartufo round ice cream covered in cocoa or chocolate
tiramisu coffee-soaked sponge, egg and Marsala
  cream and cocoa powder
torta tart, flan
tortellini small packets of pasta stuffed with pork loin,
  ham, Parmesan and nutmeg
trenette col pesto type of flat spaghetti with crushed
  basil, garlic, oil and Parmesan cheese sauce
triglia mullet
trippa tripe
trota trout
uva grapes
vongole clams
zabaione cream made from beaten eggs, sugar and
  Marsala
zafferano saffron
zucca pumkin
zucchine courgettes
zuppa soup
zuppa di cipolle onion soup
zuppa di pesce fish soup
zuppa inglese trifle

HAVING A DRINK

bar	un bar *bar*
beer	una birra *beer-ra*
coke (R)	una coca *koka*
dry	secco *sek-ko*
fresh orange	un sugo d'arancia *soogo darancha*
gin and tonic	un gin-tonic *jeen-toneek*
ice	il ghiaccio *g-yacho*
lager	una birra chiara *beer-ra k-yara*
lemonade	una gazzosa *gatsoza*
pub	un bar *bar*
red	rosso *ros-so*
straight	liscio *leesho*
sweet	dolce *dolchay*
vodka	la vodka *vodka*
whisky	un whisky *weeskee*
white	bianco *bee-anko*
wine	il vino *veeno*

let's go for a drink
andiamo a bere qualcosa?
and-yamo a bayray kwalkoza

a beer please
una birra, per piacere
oona beer-ra pair pee-achayray

two beers please
due birre, per piacere
dooay beer-ray pair pee-achayray

a glass of red/ white wine
un bicchiere di vino rosso/ bianco
oon beek-yayray dee veeno ros-so/ b-yanko

with lots of ice
con molto ghiaccio
kon molto g-yacho

25

HAVING A DRINK

no ice thanks
senza ghiaccio, per piacere
sentsa g-yacho pair pee-achayray

can I have another one?
me ne dà un altro?
may nay da oon altro

the same again please
lo stesso, per piacere
lo stes-so pair pee-achayray

what'll you have?
cosa prende?
koza prenday

I'll get this round
tocca a me
tok-ka a may

not for me thanks
non per me, grazie
non pair may gratsee-ay

he's absolutely smashed
è completamente sbronzo
ay kompletamente sbrontso

cheers!
alla salute!
al-la salootay

birra alla spina	draught beer
birra chiara	lager
birra piccola	small beer (*quarter litre*)
birra scura	brown beer
caffè	black coffee
caffè con panna	white coffee (*small cup*)
caffelatte	white coffee
listino prezzi	price list
mezza birra	third of a litre of beer
tavola calda	café-restaurant
vino bianco/ rosso	white/ red wine

COLLOQUIAL EXPRESSIONS

barmy	matto *mat-to*
bastard	bastardo *bastardo*
bird	una ragazza *ragatsa*
bloke	un tizio *teets-yo*
boozer (*pub*)	un'osteria *ostairee-a*
nutter	uno svitato *sveetato*
pissed	sbronzo *sbrontso*
thickie	un imbecille *eembecheel-lay*
twit	un cretino *kreteeno*

great!
benissimo!
baynees-seemo

that's awful!
che cosa orrenda!
kay koza or-renda!

shut up!
taci!
tachee

ouch!
ahia!
a-ya

yum-yum!
che buono!
kay bwono

I'm absolutely knackered
sono distrutto
sono deestroot-to

I'm fed up
sono stufo
sono stoofo

COLLOQUIAL EXPRESSIONS

I'm fed up with ...
ne ho piene le scatole di ...
nay o p-yaynay lay skatolay dee

don't make me laugh!
non farmi ridere!
non farmee reedairay

you've got to be joking!
vuoi scherzare!
voy skairtsaray

it's rubbish (*goods etc*)
è una porcheria!
ay oona porkairee-a

it's a rip-off
è una rapina
ay oona rapeena

get a move on!
muoviti!
mwoveetee

get lost!
vattene!
vat-tenay

it's a nuisance
è una seccaturà
ay oona sayk-katoora

it's absolutely fantastic
è fantastico!
ay fantasteeko

benissimo	great
ecco!	that's it!
guidatore della domenica!	learn to drive!
imbecille!	you idiot!
ma va'!	I don't believe it
va' all'inferno!	get lost!
va bene!	it's OK/I'm OK

GETTING AROUND

bike	una bici *beechee*
bus	l'autobus *m owtoboos*
car	una macchina *makeena*
change *(trains etc)*	cambiare *kamb-yaray*
garage	un distributore di benzina
(for fuel)	*deestreebootoray dee bentseena*
hitch-hike	fare l'autostop *fare lowtostop*
map	una carta *karta*
moped	un motorino *motoreeno*
motorbike	una moto *moto*
petrol	la benzina *bentseena*
return (ticket)	una andata e ritorno *andata ay reetorno*
single	una sola andata *sola andata*
station	la stazione *stats-yonay*
taxi	un taxi *taksee*
ticket	un biglietto *beel-yet-to*
train	il treno *trayno*
underground	la metropolitana *metropoleetana*

I'd like to rent a car/ bike/ moped
vorrei affittare una macchina/ bici/ un motorino
vor-ray af-feet-taray oona makeena/ beechee/ oon motoreeno

how much is it per day?
quanto costa al giorno?
kwanto kosta al jorno

when do I have to bring the car back?
quando devo riportare la macchina?
kwando dayvo reeportaray la makeena

I'm heading for ...
vado a ...
vado a

how do I get to ...?
come arrivo a ...?
komay ar-reevo a

REPLIES

tutto diritto
toot-to deereet-to
straight on

volti a sinistra/ a destra
voltee a seeneestra/ a destra
turn left/ right

è quell'edificio là
ay kwel edeefeecho la
it's that building there

deve tornare indietro di là
dayvay tornaray eendee-aytro dee la
it's back that way

prima/ seconda/ terza a sinistra
preema/ sekonda/ tairtza a seeneestra
first/ second/ third on the left

we're just travelling around
stiamo visitando la zona
st-yamo veezeetando la tsona

I'm a stranger here
non sono di qui
non sono dee kwee

is that on the way?
è sulla strada?
ay sool-la strada

can I get off here?
mi fa scendere qui?
mee fa shendairay kwee

thanks very much for the lift
grazie del passaggio
gratsee-ay del pas-sajo

two returns to ... please
due andata e ritorno per ... per piacere
dooay andata ay reetorno pair ... pair pee-achayray

GETTING AROUND

what time is the last train back?
a che ora parte l'ultimo treno?
a kay ora partay loolteemo trayno

we want to leave tomorrow and come back the day after
vogliamo partire domani e tornare dopodomani
vol-yamo parteeray domanee ay tornaray dopodomanee

we're coming back the same day
torneremo in giornata
tornairaymo een jornata

is this the right platform for …?
è il binario giusto per …?
ay eel beenaree-o joosto pair

is this train going to …?
è questo il treno che va a …?
ay kwesto eel trayno kay va a

which station is this?
che stazione è questa?
kay stats-yonay ay kwesta

which stop is it for …?
dove devo scendere per andare a …?
dovay dayvo shendairay pair andaray a

is there any sort of runabout ticket?
avete dei biglietti-giramondo?
avaytay day beel-yet-tee-jeeramondo

can I take my bike on the train?
posso mettere la mia bici sul treno?
pos-so met-tairay la mee-a beechee sool trayno

how far is it to the nearest petrol station?
dov'è il distributore di benzina più vicino?
dovay eel deestreebootoray dee bentseena p-yoo veecheeno

I need a new tyre
ho bisogno di un pneumatico nuovo
o beezon-yo dee oon noomateeko nwovo

it's overheating
il motore surriscalda
eel motore soor-reeskalda

there's something wrong with the brakes
i freni non funzionano molto bene
ee fraynee non foonts-yonano molto baynay

arrivi	arrival(s)
autostrada	motorway
biglietteria	ticket office
binario	platform
dare la precedenza	give way
deviazione	diversion
distributore automatico di biglietti	ticket machine
divieto di sosta	no parking
è vietato usare la toilette quando il treno è in stazione	do not use the toilet while the train is in a station
fine di ...	end of ...
galleria	tunnel
giorni dispari/ pari (sosta permessa nei ...)	odd/ even dates of the month (parking allowed)
lasciare libero il passaggio	no parking please
lavori stradali	roadworks
Metropolitana	underground
normale	2 star petrol
partenza/ partenze	departure/ departures
passo	pass
pedaggio	toll
precedenza a destra	vehicles coming from the right have priority
senza piombo	lead-free
stazione degli autobus	bus station
super	4 star petrol
viadotto	bridge, viaduct
vietato sporgersi dal finestrino	do not lean out of the window
zona di parcheggio limitato	restricted parking area in town centre

SHOPPING

carrier bag	una borsa *borsa*
cashdesk	la cassa *kas-sa*
cheap	a buon mercato *a bwon mairkato*
cheque	un assegno *a-sen-yo*
department	il reparto *rayparto*
expensive	caro *karo*
pay	pagare *pagaray*
receipt	una ricevuta *reechayvoota*
shop	un negozio *naygots-yo*
shop	il commesso, *kom-mes-so,*
assistant	la commessa *kom-mes-sa*
supermarket	il supermercato *soopairmairkato*
till	la cassa *kas-sa*

I'd like ...
vorrei ...
vor-ray

have you got ...?
avete ...?
av-ay-tay

how much is this?
quanto costa questo?
kwanto kosta kwesto

can I just have a look around?
posso dare un'occhiata?
pos-so daray oonok-yata

the one in the window
quello in vetrina
kwel-lo een vetreena

do you take credit cards?
accettate le carte di credito?
achet-tatay lay kartay dee kraydeeto

33

SHOPPING

could I have a receipt please?
vorrei la ricevuta
vor-ray la reechayvoota

I'd like to try it on
vorrei provarlo
vor-ray provarlo

I'll come back
tornerò
tornairo

it's too big/ small
è troppo grande/ piccolo
ay trop-po granday/ peekolo

it's not what I'm looking for
non è quello che cercavo
non ay kwel-lo kay chairkavo

I'll take it
lo prendo
lo prendo

can you gift-wrap it?
può farmi una confezione regalo?
pwo farmee oona konfets-yonay regalo

abiti	clothes
alimentari	food
cassa	till
chiuso	closed
da consumarsi entro . . .	best before . . .
da vendersi entro . . .	sell-by date
munirsi di carrello	take a trolley
orario d'apertura	opening times
pagare alla cassa	pay at the desk
saldi	sale
sali e tabacchi	salt and tobacco
sconto	reduction
tenere in luogo fresco	keep in a cool place

ITALY AND THINGS ITALIAN

Some names which are different:

Capitol Hill	il Campidoglio *kampeedolyo*
Coliseum	il Colosseo *kolossay-o*
Florence	Firenze *feerentsay*
Genoa	Genova *jenova*
Milan	Milano *meelano*
Naples	Napoli *napolee*
Padua	Padova *padova*
Roman Forum	il Foro Romano *foro romano*
Rome	Roma *roma*
Sardinia	Sardegna *sardaynya*
Sicily	Sicilia *seecheelya*
St. Peter's	San Pietro *san pyaytro*
Tiber	il Tevere *tayvayray*
Turin	Torino *toreeno*
Tuscany	Toscana *toskana*
Vatican City	la Città del Vaticano *cheeta del vateekano*
Venice	Venezia *venaytsee-a*

Autostrada dei Fiori	motorway from Genoa to La Spezia
Autostrada dei Laghi	motorway from Milan to the lakes
Autostrada del Sole	motorway from Milan to Reggio di Calabria
centro storico	old town centre with places of historical interest
ENIT, EPT	tourist organizations
Ferragosto	15th August, a national holiday
il Mezzogiorno	the South
il Palio di Siena	horse race in medieval costume held in main square of Siena
Ponte dei Sospiri	The Bridge of Sighs in Venice
Riviera ligure	Italian Riviera
la Torre di Pisa	The Leaning Tower of Pisa
TCI	Touring Club Italiano

MONEY

bank	una banca *banka*
bill	il conto *konto*
bureau de change	un ufficio di cambio *oof-feecho dee kamb-yo*
cash dispenser	la cassa continua *kas-sa konteenoo-a*
change (*small*)	la moneta *monayta*
cheque	un assegno *as-sen-yo*
credit card	una carta di credito *karta dee kraydeeto*
Eurocheque	un eurocheque *yoorochek*
exchange rate	il tasso del cambio *tas-so del kamb-yo*
expensive	caro *karo*
Italian lire	le lire italiane *leeray eetalyanay*
pounds (sterling)	le lire sterline *leeray stairleenay*
price	il prezzo *pretso*
receipt	una ricevuta *reechayvoota*
traveller's cheque	un travellers' cheque *'travellers cheque'*

how much is it?
quanto costa?
kwanto kosta

I'd like to change this into ...
vorrei cambiare questi soldi in ...
vor-ray kamb-yaray kwestee soldee een

can you give me something smaller?
potrebbe darmi della moneta?
potrayb-bay darmee del-la monayta

can I use this credit card?
accettate questa carta di credito?
achet-tatay kwesta karta dee kraydeeto

can we have the bill please?
il conto, per piacere
eel konto pair pee-achayray

MONEY

please keep the change
tenga il resto
tenga eel resto

does that include service?
il servizio è compreso?
eel sairveets-yo ay komprayzo

what are your rates?
qual è la vostra tariffa?
kwalay la vostra tareef-fa

I think the figures are wrong
credo che ci sia un errore
kraydo kay chee see-a oon air-roray

I'm completely skint
sono in bolletta
sono een bol-let-ta

The unit is the 'lira' *leera*, plural 'lire' *leeray*. A
colloquial word for money is 'la grana'.

banca	bank
banca/banco di	savings bank
risparmio	
cambio	change, exchange rate
carta di credito	credit card
IVA	VAT
lira sterlina	pound sterling
prezzo d'acquisto	buying rate
prezzo di vendita	selling rate
tasso del cambio	exchange rate

band (*pop*)	il gruppo *groop-po*
cinema	il cinema *cheenayma*
concert	un concerto *konchairto*
disco	una discoteca *deeskoteka*
film	un film *feelm*
go out	uscire *oosheeray*
music	la musica *moozeeka*
night out	una serata *sayrata*
play (*theatre*)	un dramma *drama*
seat	un posto (a sedere) *posto (a saydayray)*
show	uno spettacolo *spet-takolo*
singer	un/ una cantante *kantantay*
theatre	il teatro *tay-atro*
ticket	un biglietto *beel-yet-to*

are you doing anything tonight?
che cosa fai stasera?
kay koza f eye' stasayra

do you want to come out with me tonight?
vuoi uscire (con me), stasera?
vwoy oosheeray (kon may) stasayra

what's on?
che cosa danno?
kay koza dan-no

have you got a programme of what's on in town?
avete un programma degli spettacoli in città?
avaytay oon program-ma del-yee spet-takolee een cheet-ta

which is the best disco round here?
qual è la miglior discoteca dei dintorni?
kwalay la meel-yor deeskoteka day deentornee

let's go to the cinema/ theatre
andiamo al cinema/ al teatro
and-yamo al cheenayma/ al tay-atro

ENTERTAINMENT

I've seen it
l'ho già visto
lo ja veesto

I'll meet you at 9 o'clock at the station
ci troviamo alle 9 alla stazione
chee trovee-yamo al-lay novay al-la stats-yonay

can I have two tickets for tonight's performance?
vorrei due biglietti per stasera
vor-ray dooay beel-yet-tee pair stasairah

do you want to dance?
vuoi ballare?
vwoy bal-laray

do you want to dance again?
vuoi fare un altro ballo?
vwoy faray oon altro bal-lo

thanks but I'm with my boyfriend
grazie, ma sono qui col mio amico
gratsee-ay ma sono kwee kol mee-o ameeko

let's go out for some fresh air
usciamo a prendere un po' d'aria
oosh-yamo a prendayray oon po dar-ya

will you let me back in again later?
mi lasciate rientrare quando torno?
mee lashatay ree-entraray kwando torno

I'm meeting someone inside
mi devo incontrare con una persona dentro
mee dayvo eenkontraray con oona pairsona dentro

annullato	cancelled
chiuso	closed
con sottotitoli	with subtitles
il prossimo	next showing at 8 pm
spettacolo alle 20	
in lingua originale	in the original language
sospeso	postponed

THE BEACH

beach	la spiaggia *spee-aja*
beach umbrella	un ombrellone *ombrel-lonay*
bikini	un bikini *beekeenee*
dive	tuffarsi *toof-farsee*
sand	la sabbia *sab-b-ya*
sea	il mare *maray*
sunbathe	fare i bagni di sole *faray ee ban-yee dee solay*
suntan lotion	il latte solare *lat-tay solaray*
suntan oil	l'olio solare *m ol-yo solaray*
swim	nuotare *nwotaray*
swimming costume	un costume da bagno *kostoomay da ban-yo*
tan	l'abbronzatura *f ab-brontsatoora*
towel	un asciugamano *ashoogamano*
wave	l'onda *f onda*

let's go down to the beach
andiamo in spiaggia
and-yamo een sp-eeaja

what's the water like?
com'è l'acqua?
komay lakwa

it's freezing
è gelida
ay jeleeda

it's beautiful
è bello
ay bel-lo

are you coming for a swim?
viene a fare il bagno?
vee-aynay a faray eel banyo

40

THE BEACH

I can't swim
non so nuotare
non so nwotaray

he swims like a fish
nuota come un pesce
nwota komay oon peshay

will you keep an eye on my things for me?
mi può tener d'occhio le mie cose?
mee pwo tenair dok-yo lay mee-ay kozay

is it deep here?
è fonda l'acqua?
ay fonda lakwa

could you rub suntan oil on my back?
mi può spalmare l'olio solare sulla schiena?
mee pwo spalmaray lol-yo solaray sool-la sk-yayna

I love sun bathing
adoro i bagni di sole
adoro ee ban-yee dee solay

I'm all sunburnt
mi sono preso una bella scottata
mee sono prayzo oona bel-la skot-tata

you're all wet!
sei fradicio!
say fradeecho

let's go up to the café
andiamo al caffè
and-yamo al kaf-fay

. . . a nolo	. . . for hire
bagnino	lifeguard
da affittare/noleggiare	for hire
docce	showers
è pericoloso bagnarsi	it is dangerous to swim here
è proibito bagnarsi	no swimming
gelati	ice creams

PROBLEMS

accident	un incidente *eencheedentay*
ambulance	un'ambulanza *amboolantsa*
broken	rotto *rot-to*
doctor	un medico *maydeeko*
emergency	un'emergenza *emairjentsa*
fire	un incendio *eenchend-yo*
fire brigade	i pompieri *pomp-yayree*
ill	malato *malato*
injured	ferito *faireeto*
late	in ritardo *een reetardo*
out of order	guasto *gwasto*
police	la polizia *poleetsee-a*

can you help me? I'm lost
può aiutarmi? mi sono perso
pwo ayootarmee? mee sono pairso

I've lost my passport
ho perso il passaporto
o pairso eel pas-saporto

I've locked myself out of my room
mi sono chiuso fuori della mia camera
mee sono kyoozo fworee del-la mee-a kamaira

my luggage hasn't arrived
il mio bagaglio non è arrivato
eel mee-o bagal-yo non ay ar-reevato

I can't get it open
non riesco ad aprire
non ree-aysko ad apreeray

it's jammed
è bloccato
ay blok-kato

PROBLEMS

I don't have enough money
non ho abbastanza soldi
non o ab-bastantsa soldee

I've broken down
ho avuto un guasto
o avooto oon gwasto

can I use your telephone please, this is an emergency
posso usare il vostro telefono? si tratta di una
questione d'emergenza
pos-so oozaray eel vostro taylayfono see trat-ta dee oona
kwest-yonay demairjentsa

help!
aiuto!
a-yooto

it doesn't work
non funziona
non foonts-yona

the lights aren't working in my room
nella mia stanza non s'accende la luce
nel-la mee-a stantsa non sachenday la loochay

the lift is stuck
l'ascensore è bloccato
lashensoray ay blok-kato

I can't understand a single word
non capisco niente
non kapeesko n-yentay

can you get an interpreter?
può trovare un interprete?
pwo trovaray oon eentairpraytay

the toilet won't flush
lo sciacquone del gabinetto non funziona
lo shakonay del gabeenet-to non foonts-yona

there's no plug in the bath
non c'è il tappo nella vasca da bagno
non chay eel tap-po nel-la vaska da ban-yo

PROBLEMS

there's no hot water
non c'è acqua calda
non chay akwa kalda

there's no toilet paper left
non c'è più carta igienica
non chay p-yoo karta eejayneeka

I'm afraid I've accidentally broken the ...
mi rincresce molto, ho rotto il/ la ...
mee reenkrayshay molto o rot-to eel/ la ...

this man has been following me
quest'uomo mi segue da un po'
kwestwomo mee segway da oon po

I've been mugged
sono stato(a) assalito(a)
sono stato(a) as-saleeto(a)

my handbag has been stolen
mi hanno rubato la borsetta
mee an-no roobato la borset-ta

attenti al cane	beware of the dog
attenzione	caution
fuori servizio	out of order
guasto	out of order
pronto soccorso	emergency, police (999)
polizia	
proibito ...	no ...
ufficio oggetti smarriti	lost property office
uscita d'emergenza	emergency exit
vietato	prohibited

bandage	la benda *benda*
blood	il sangue *san-gway*
broken	rotto *rot-to*
burn	la bruciatura *broochatoora*
chemist's	la farmacia *farmachee-a*
contraception	la contraccezione *kontrachets-yonay*
dentist	un dentista *denteesta*
disabled	invalido *eenvaleedo*
disease	una malattia *malat-tee-a*
doctor	un medico *maydeeko*
health	la salute *salootay*
hospital	l'ospedale *m ospedalay*
ill	malato *malato*
nurse	un'infermiera *eenfairm-yayra*
wound	una ferita *faireeta*

I don't feel well
non mi sento bene
non mee sento baynay

it's getting worse
peggiora
pejora

I feel better
mi sento meglio
mee sento mel-yo

I feel sick
ho la nausea
o la nows-ay-a

I've got a pain here
ho un dolore qui
o oon doloray kwee

it hurts
fa male
fa malay

HEALTH

he's got a high temperature
ha la febbre alta
a la feb-bray alta

could you call a doctor?
può chiamare un medico?
pwo k-yamaray oon maydeeko

is it serious?
è grave?
ay gravay

will he need an operation?
ha bisogno di essere operato?
a beezon-yo dee es-sairay opairato

I'm diabetic
sono diabetico
sono dee-abeteeko

keep her warm
la tenga al caldo
la ten-ga al kaldo

have you got anything for ...?
avete qualcosa per ...?
avaytay kwalkoza pair

agitare prima dell'uso	shake before use
da non ingerirsi	not to be taken internally
da prendere a digiuno	to be taken on an empty stomach
da prendere prima/ dopo i pasti	to be taken before/ after meals
da vendersi solo dietro presentazione di ricetta medica	sold on prescription only
pronto soccorso	emergency medical service
sciogliere	dissolve
studio medico	doctor's surgery
tranquillante	tranquillizer
una compressa al giorno	one tablet a day

SPORT

I want to learn to sailboard
voglio imparare ad andare con la tavola da vela
vol-yo eempararay ad andaray kon la tavola da vayla

can we hire a sailing boat?
possiamo affittare una barca a vela?
pos-s-yamo af-feet-taray oona barka a vayla

how much is half an hour's waterskiing?
quanto costa mezz'ora di sci d'acqua?
kwanto kosta metsora dee shee dakwa

I'd like lessons in skin-diving
vorrei prendere lezioni di nuoto subacqueo
vor-ray prendairay lets-yonee dee nwoto soobakway-o

can we use the tennis court?
possiamo usare il campo da tennis?
pos-syamo oozaray eel kampo da ten-nees

how much is a skipass?
quanto costa uno ski-pass?
kwanto kosta oono skee-pass

I'd like to go and watch a football match
vorrei andare a vedere una partita di calcio
vor-ray andaray a vaydayray oona parteeta dee kalcho

is it possible to do any horse-riding here?
si può andare a cavallo qui?
see pwo andaray a kaval-lo kwee

we're going to do some hill-walking
andiamo a fare delle passeggiate in montagna
and-yamo a faray del-lay pas-say-jatay een montanya

this is the first time I've ever tried it
questa è la prima volta che lo (la) provo
kwesta ay la preema volta kay lo (la) provo

47

THE POST OFFICE

letter	la lettera *let-taira*
parcel	il pacco *pak-ko*
poste restante	fermo-posta *fairmoposta*
post office	l'ufficio postale *oof-feecho postalay*
recorded delivery	raccomandata *rak-komandata*
send	mandare *mandaray*
stamp	un francobollo *frankobol-lo*
telegram	un telegramma *telegram-ma*

how much is a letter to Ireland?
quanto costa un francobollo per lettera per l'Irlanda?
kwanto kosta oon frankobol-lo pair let-taira pair leerlanda

I'd like four 600 lire stamps
vorrei quattro francobolli da seicento lire
vor-ray kwat-tro frankobol-lee da say-chento leeray

I'd like six stamps for postcards to England
vorrei sei francobolli per cartolina per l'Inghilterra
vor-ray say frankobol-lee pair kartoleena pair leengeeltair-ra

is there any mail for me?
c'è posta per me?
chay posta pair may

I'm expecting a parcel from . . .
aspetto un pacco da . . .
aspet-to oon pak-ko da

codice d'avviamento postale	post code
destinatario	addressee
francobolli	stamps
mittente	sender
poste e telegrafi, PT	post office and telephones
prossima levata	next collection

directory enquiries	informazioni elenco abbonati *eenformats-yonee aylenko ab-bonatee*
engaged	occupato *ok-koopato*
extension	l'interno *m eentairno*
number	il numero *noomairo*
operator	il centralino *chentraleeno*
phone (*verb*)	telefonare *telefonaray*
phone box	una cabina telefonica *kabeena telefoneeka*
telephone	il telefono *telefono*
telephone directory	l'elenco del telefono *m elenko del telefono*

is there a phone round here?
c'è un telefono nei dintorni?
chay oon telefono nay deentorno

can I use your phone?
posso usare il suo telefono?
pos-so oozaray eel soo-o telefono

I'd like to make a phone call to Britain
vorrei telefonare in Gran Bretagna
vor-ray telefonaray een gran bretan-ya

I want to reverse the charges
vorrei fare una chiamata a carico del destinatario
vor-ray faray oona k-yamata a kareeko del desteenatar-yo

hello
pronto?
pronto

could I speak to Patricia?
vorrei parlare con Patricia
vor-ray parlaray kon Patricia

hello, this is Simon speaking
pronto, qui parla Simon
pronto kwee parla Simon

TELEPHONING

can I leave a message?
potrei lasciare un messaggio?
potr-ay lasharay oon mes-sajo

do you speak English?
parla inglese?
parla eenglayzay

could you say that again very very slowly?
potrebbe ripetere molto lentamente?
potrayb-bay reepetayray molto lentamentay

could you tell him Jim called?
potrebbe dirgli che ha chiamato Jim?
potrayb-bay deerl-yee kay a k-yamato Jim

could you ask her to ring me back?
potrebbe chiederle di richiamarmi?
potrayb-bay k-yaydairlay dee reek-yamarmee

I'll call back later
richiamo più tardi
reek-yamo p-yoo tardee

my number is . . .
il mio numero è . . .
eel mee-o noomairo ay

776-3211
sette sette sei − tre due uno uno
set-tay set-tay say tray doo-ay oono oono

just a minute please
un attimo, prego
oon at-teemo praygo

he's not in
non c'è
non chay

sorry, I've got the wrong number
spiacente, ho sbagliato numero
spee-achentay o sbal-yato noomairo

it's a terrible line
la linea è pessima
la leen-ya ay pes-seema

TELEPHONING

REPLIES

aspetti
aspet-tee
hang on

chi devo dire?
kee dayvo deeray
who shall I say is calling?

chi parla?
kee parla
who's speaking?

chiamate il ...	dial ...
gettoni	telephone tokens
guida telefonica	phone book
il numero di questa cabina è ...	incoming calls can be made to the following number: ...
pompieri	fire brigade
segnale della centrale	(ringing) tone
telefono per interurbane	long-distance phone

THE ALPHABET

how do you spell it?
come si scrive?
komay see skreevay

I'll spell it
si scrive ...
see skreevay

a	*ah*	g	*gee*	m	*em-may*	s	*es-say*	y	*ee-grayka*
b	*bee*	h	*ak-ka*	n	*en-nay*	t	*tee*	z	*tsay-ta*
c	*chee*	i	*ee*	o	*oh*	u	*oo*	
d	*dee*	j	*ee loonga*	p	*pee*	v	*voo*	
e	*ay*	k	*kap-pa*	q	*koo*	w	*voo dop-pyo*	
f	*ef-fay*	l	*el-lay*	r	*air-ray*	x	*eeks*	

NUMBERS, THE DATE, THE TIME

0	zero *tsayro*
1	uno *oono*
2	due *doo-ay*
3	tre *tray*
4	quattro *kwat-tro*
5	cinque *cheenkway*
6	sei *say*
7	sette *set-tay*
8	otto *ot-to*
9	nove *novay*
10	dieci *dee-aychee*
11	undici *oondeechee*
12	dodici *dodeechee*
13	tredici *traydeechee*
14	quattordici *kwat-tordeechee*
15	quindici *kweendeechee*
16	sedici *saydeechee*
17	diciassette *deechas-set-tay*
18	diciotto *deechot-to*
19	diciannove *deechanovay*
20	venti *ventee*
21	ventuno *ventoono*
22	ventidue *venteedoo-ay*
30	trenta *trenta*
31	trentuno *trentoono*
32	trentadue *trentadooay*
40	quaranta *kwaranta*
50	cinquanta *cheenkwanta*
60	sessanta *ses-santa*
70	settanta *set-tanta*
80	ottanta *ot-tanta*
90	novanta *novanta*
100	cento *chento*

NUMBERS, THE DATE, THE TIME

101	centouno *chento-oono*
102	centodue *chentodoo-ay*
200	duecento *doo-aychento*
300	trecento *traychento*

1,000	mille *meel-lay*
2,000	duemila *doo-aymeela*
5,000	cinquemila *cheenkwaymeela*

1,000,000	un milione *oon meel-yonay*
2,000,000	due milioni *doo-ay meel-yonee*

1st	primo *preemo*
2nd	secondo *sekondo*
3rd	terzo *tairtzo*
4th	quarto *kwarto*
5th	quinto *kweento*
6th	sesto *sesto*
7th	settimo *set-teemo*
8th	ottavo *ot-tavo*
9th	nono *nono*
10th	decimo *daycheemo*

what's the date?
che giorno è?
kay jorno ay

it's the 1st/ 12th of January 1994
è il primo/ dodici gennaio
millenovecentonovantaquattro
ay eel preemo/ dodeechee jen-na-yo
meel-lay-novaychento-novantakwatro

what time is it?
che ora è ?
kay ora ay

it's midday/ midnight
è mezzogiorno/ mezzanotte
ay metsojorno/ metsanot-tay

it's one/ three o'clock
è l'una/ sono le tre
ay loona/ sono lay tray

53

NUMBERS, THE DATE, THE TIME

it's half past eight
sono le otto e mezza
sono lay ot-to ay metsa

it's a quarter past/ to five
sono le cinque e un quarto/ meno un quarto
sono lay cheenkway ay oon kwarto/ mayno oon kwarto

it's six a.m./ p.m.
sono le sei di mattina/ di sera
sono lay say dee mat-teena/ dee sayra

at two/ five p.m.
alle quattordici/ diciassette
al-lay kwat-tordeechee/ deechas-set-tay

ENGLISH-ITALIAN

A

a uno, *f* una (*see grammar*)
about (*approx*) circa
above sopra
abroad all'estero
accelerator l'acceleratore *m*
accent l'accento *m*
accept accettare
accident l'incidente *m*
accommodation l'alloggio *m*
accompany accompagnare
ache il dolore
adaptor il riduttore
address l'indirizzo *m*
address book la rubrica
adult l'adulto *m*
advance: in advance in anticipo
advise consigliare
aeroplane l'aeroplano *m*
afraid: I'm afraid (of) ho paura (di)
after dopo
afternoon il pomeriggio
aftershave il dopobarba
afterwards dopo
again di nuovo
against contro
age l'età *f*
agency l'agenzia *f*
agent il rappresentante; (*for cars*) il concessionario
aggressive aggressivo

ago: three days ago tre giorni fa
agree: I agree sono d'accordo
AIDS l'aids *m*
air l'aria *f*
air-conditioned con aria condizionata
air-conditioning l'aria condizionata *f*
air hostess l'hostess *f*
airline la linea aerea
airmail: by airmail posta aerea
airport l'aeroporto *m*
alarm l'allarme *m*
alarm clock la sveglia
alcohol l'alcool *m*
alive vivo
all: all men/ women tutti gli uomini/ tutte le donne; **all the milk/ beer** tutto il latte/ tutta la birra; **all day** tutto il giorno
allergic to allergico a
all-inclusive tutto compreso
allow permettere
allowed permesso
all right: that's all right d'accordo
almost quasi
alone solo
Alps gli Alpi
already già
also anche
alternator l'alternatore *m*
although sebbene
altogether in tutto

always sempre
a.m.: at 5 a.m. alle 5 del mattino
ambulance l'ambulanza *f*
America l'America *f*
American americano
among tra
amp: 15-amp da 15 ampère
ancestor l'antenato *m*
anchor l'ancora *f*
ancient antico
and e
angina l'angina pectoris *f*
angry arrabbiato
animal l'animale *m*
ankle la caviglia
anniversary (*wedding*) l'anniversario di matrimonio *m*
annoying seccante
anorak la giacca a vento
another un altro, *f* un'altra
answer la risposta
answer (*verb*) rispondere
ant la formica
antibiotic l'antibiotico *m*
antifreeze l'antigelo *m*
antihistamine l'antistaminico *m*
antique: it's an antique è un pezzo d'antiquariato
antique shop il negozio di antiquariato
antiseptic antisettico
any: have you got any butter/bananas? avete del burro/delle banane?; **I don't have any** non ne ho
anyway in ogni caso
apartment l'appartamento *m*
aperitif l'aperitivo *m*
apologize scusarsi
appalling spaventoso

appendicitis l'appendicite *f*
appetite l'appetito *m*
apple la mela
apple pie la crostata di mele
appointment l'appuntamento *m*
apricot l'albicocca *f*
April aprile
archaeology l'archeologia *f*
area la zona
arm il braccio
arrest arrestare
arrival l'arrivo *m*
arrive arrivare
art l'arte *f*
art gallery la galleria d'arte
artificial artificiale
artist l'artista *m/f*
as (*since*) siccome; **as beautiful as** bello come
ashamed pieno di vergogna
ashtray il portacenere
ask chiedere
asleep addormentato
asparagus gli asparagi
aspirin l'aspirina *f*
asthma l'asma *f*
astonishing stupefacente
at: at the station alla stazione; **at Betty's** da Betty; **at 3 o'clock** alle tre
Atlantic l'Atlantico *m*
attractive attraente
aubergine la melanzana
audience il pubblico
August agosto
aunt la zia
Australia l'Australia *f*
Australian australiano
Austria l'Austria *f*
Austrian austriaco
automatic automatico
autumn l'autunno *m*

awake sveglio
awful terribile
axe l'ascia f
axle il semiasse

B

baby il bebè
baby-sitter il/ la baby-sitter
bachelor lo scapolo
back il dietro; (of body) la
  schiena; the back wheel/
  seat la ruota/ il sedile
  posteriore
backpack lo zaino
bacon la pancetta
bad cattivo
badly male
bag la borsa
bake cuocere al forno
baker's il fornaio
balcony il balcone
bald calvo
ball la palla
banana la banana
bandage la fasciatura
bank la banca
bar il bar
barbecue il barbecue
barber il barbiere
barmaid la cameriera
barman il barman
basement il seminterrato
basket il cestino
bath il bagno
bathing cap la cuffia da
  bagno
bathroom il bagno
bath salts i sali da bagno
bathtub la vasca da bagno
battery la batteria

be essere (see grammar)
beach la spiaggia
beans i fagioli; green beans
  i fagiolini verdi
beard la barba
beautiful bello
because perché
become diventare
bed il letto; single/ double
  bed letto a una piazza/ due
  piazze; go to bed andare a
  letto
bed linen la biancheria da
  letto
bedroom la camera da letto
bee l'ape f
beef il manzo
beer la birra
before prima; before
  tomorrow prima di domani
begin cominciare
beginner il principiante
beginning l'inizio m
behind dietro (a)
beige beige
Belgian belga
Belgium il Belgio
believe credere
bell la campana; (for door) il
  campanello
belong appartenere
below sotto
belt la cintura
bend la curva
best migliore
better meglio
between fra
bicycle la bicicletta
big grande
bikini il bikini
bill il conto
bird l'uccello m
biro (R) la biro

birthday il compleanno;
  happy birthday! buon
  compleanno!
biscuit il biscotto
bit: a little bit un po'
bite il morso; (*insect*) la
  puntura
bitter amaro
black nero
black and white bianco e
  nero
blackberry la mora
bladder la vescica
blanket la coperta
bleach la varechina
bleed sanguinare
bless you! salute!
blind cieco
blister la vescica
blocked bloccato
blond biondo
blood il sangue
blood group il gruppo
  sanguigno
blouse la camicetta
blow-dry l'asciugatura con
  föhn *f*
blue azzurro
boarding pass la carta
  d'imbarco
boat la nave
body il corpo
boil bollire
bolt il catenaccio
bolt (*verb*) chiudere con il
  catenaccio
bomb la bomba
bone l'osso *m*
bonnet (*car*) il cofano
book il libro
book (*verb*) prenotare
bookshop la libreria
boot (*shoe*) lo stivale; (*car*) il

bagagliaio
border il confine
boring noioso
born: I was born in 1963 sono
  nato nel 1963
borrow prendere a prestito
boss il capo
both: both of them tutti e due
bottle la bottiglia
bottle-opener
  l'apribottiglie *m*
bottom il fondo; (*of body*) il
  sedere; **at the bottom of** in
  fondo a
bowl la scodella
box la scatola
box office il botteghino
boy il ragazzo
boyfriend il ragazzo
bra il reggiseno
bracelet il braccialetto
brake il freno
brake (*verb*) frenare
brandy il brandy
brave coraggioso
bread il pane; **white/
  wholemeal bread** pane
  bianco/ integrale
break rompere
break down restare in panne
breakdown (*car*) il guasto;
  (*nervous*) l'esaurimento
  nervoso *m*
breakfast la colazione
breast il seno
breastfeed allattare al seno
breathe respirare
brick il mattone
bridge (*over river*) il ponte
briefcase la cartella
bring portare
Britain la Gran Bretagna
British britannico

brochure l'opuscolo m
broke: I'm broke sono al verde
broken rotto
brooch la spilla
broom la scopa
brother il fratello
brother-in-law il cognato
brown marrone
bruise il livido
brush la spazzola
Brussels sprouts i cavoletti di Bruxelles
bucket il secchio
building l'edificio m
bulb (light) la lampadina
bumper il paraurti
bunk beds i letti a castello
buoy la boa
burn la scottatura
burn (verb) bruciare
bus l'autobus m
business gli affari
business trip il viaggio d'affari
bus station la stazione degli autobus
bus stop la fermata dell'autobus
busy occupato
but ma
butcher's la macelleria
butter il burro
butterfly la farfalla
button il bottone
buy comprare
by da; by car in macchina; by sea per mare

cabbage il cavolo
cabin (ship) la cabina
cable car la funivia
café il bar
cagoule la giacca a vento
cake la torta
cake shop la pasticceria
calculator il calcolatore
calendar il calendario
call chiamare
calm down calmarsi
Calor gas (R) il butano
camera (still) la macchina fotografica; (movie) la macchina da presa
campbed la branda
camping il campeggio
campsite il campeggio
can la lattina
can: I/ she can posso/ può; can you? può?
Canada il Canadà
Canadian canadese
canal il canale
cancel annullare
candle la candela
canoe la canoa
cap il berretto
captain il capitano
car la macchina
caravan la roulotte
caravan site il campeggio per roulotte
carburettor il carburatore
card (playing) la carta; (birthday etc) la cartolina; (business) il biglietto da visita
cardboard il cartone

ENGLISH-ITALIAN

cardigan il golf aperto
car driver l'automobilista m
care: take care of prendersi
  cura di
careful attento; be careful!
  faccia attenzione!
car park il parcheggio
carpet il tappeto
car rental il noleggio di
  automobili
carriage la carrozza
carrot la carota
carry portare
carry-cot il porte-enfant
cash: pay cash pagare in
  contante
cash desk la cassa
cash dispenser lo sportello
  automatico
cassette la cassetta
cassette player il
  mangianastri
castle il castello
cat il gatto
catch prendere
cathedral la cattedrale
Catholic cattolico
cauliflower il cavolfiore
cause la causa
cave la grotta
ceiling il soffitto
cemetery il cimitero
centigrade centigrado
central heating il
  riscaldamento centrale
centre il centro
century il secolo
certificate il certificato
chain la catena
chair la sedia
chairlift la seggiovia
chambermaid la cameriera
chance: by chance per caso

change (small) gli spiccioli
change (verb) cambiare;
  (clothes) cambiarsi; change
  trains cambiare treno
changeable (weather)
  variabile
Channel la Manica
charter flight il volo charter
cheap a buon mercato
check (verb) controllare
check-in il check-in
cheers! alla salute!
cheese il formaggio
chemist's la farmacia
cheque l'assegno m
cheque book il libretto degli
  assegni
cheque card la carta assegni
cherry la ciliegia
chest il petto
chestnut la castagna
chewing gum il chewing-
  gum
chicken il pollo
child, pl children il bambino
children's portion la
  porzione per bambini
chin il mento
chips le patatine fritte
chocolate il cioccolato; milk/
  plain chocolate cioccolato
  al latte/ fondente; hot
  chocolate la cioccolata calda
choke lo starter
choose scegliere
chop (meat) la costoletta
Christian name il nome di
  battesimo
Christmas il Natale; Happy
  Christmas Buon Natale
church la chiesa
cider il sidro
cigar il sigaro

60

ENGLISH-ITALIAN

cigarette la sigaretta
cinema il cinema
city la città
city centre il centro della città
class la classe; first/ second class la prima/ seconda classe
classical music la musica classica
clean pulito
clean (verb) pulire
cleansing cream la crema detergente
clear chiaro
clever intelligente
cliff la scogliera
climate il clima
cloakroom (for coats) il guardaroba
clock l'orologio m
close (verb) chiudere
closed chiuso
clothes gli abiti
clothes peg la molletta da bucato
cloud la nuvola
cloudy nuvoloso
club il club
clutch la frizione
coach la corriera
coast la costa
coat il cappotto
coathanger la gruccia
cockroach lo scarafaggio
cocktail il cocktail
cocoa il cacao
coffee il caffè; white coffee il caffellatte
cold freddo; it is cold fà freddo
cold (illness) il raffreddore
cold cream la crema di bellezza

collar il colletto
collection la collezione
colour il colore; colour film la pellicola a colori
comb il pettine
come venire; I come from London sono di Londra; come back tornare; come in! avanti!
comfortable comodo
compact disc il compactdisc
company la ditta
compartment lo scompartimento
compass la bussola
complain lamentarsi
complicated complicato
compliment il complimento
computer il computer
concert il concerto
conditioner la crema doposhampoo
condom il preservativo
conductor (bus) il bigliettaio
confirm dare conferma
congratulations! congratulazioni!
connection (travel) la coincidenza
constipated stitico
consulate il consolato
contact (verb) mettersi in contatto con
contact lenses le lenti a contatto
contraceptive il contraccettivo
cook il cuoco
cook (verb) cucinare
cooker la cucina
cooking utensils gli utensili da cucina
cool fresco

corkscrew il cavatappi
corner l'angolo m
correct esatto
corridor il corridoio
cosmetics i cosmetici
cost costare
cot il lettino
cotton il cotone
cotton wool il cotone idrofilo
couchette la cuccetta
cough la tosse
cough (verb) tossire
country il paese
countryside la campagna
course: of course
  naturalmente
cousin il cugino, la cugina
cow la mucca
crab il granchio
crafts l'artigianato m
cramp il crampo
crankshaft l'albero a
  gomiti m
crash l'incidente m
crayfish il gambero
cream la panna
credit card la carta di credito
crew l'equipaggio m
crisps le patatine
crockery il vasellame
cross (verb) attraversare
crowd la folla
crowded affollato
cruise la crociera
crutches le stampelle
cry piangere
cucumber il cetriolo
cup la tazza
cupboard l'armadietto m
curry il curry
curtain la tenda
custom (of area) la tradizione
customs la dogana

cut (verb) tagliare
cutlery le posate
cycling il ciclismo
cyclist il ciclista
cylinder head gasket la
  guarnizione della testata

dad il papà
damage (verb) danneggiare
damp umido
dance (verb) ballare
danger il pericolo
dangerous pericoloso
dare osare
dark scuro
dashboard il cruscotto
date (time) la data
daughter la figlia
daughter-in-law la nuora
day il giorno; the day before
  yesterday l'altroieri; the
  day after tomorrow
  dopodomani
dead morto
deaf sordo
dear caro
death la morte
decaffeinated decaffeinato
December dicembre
decide decidere
deck il ponte di coperta
deck chair la sedia a sdraio
deep profondo
delay il ritardo
deliberately volutamente
delicious delizioso
dentist il dentista
dentures la dentiera
deodorant il deodorante

department store il grande magazzino
departure la partenza
depend: it depends dipende
depressed depresso
dessert il dolce
develop sviluppare
device il dispositivo
diabetic diabetico
dialect il dialetto
dialling code il prefisso
diamond il diamante
diarrhoea la diarrea
diary il diario
dictionary il dizionario
die morire
diesel (*fuel*) il diesel
diet la dieta
different diverso
difficult difficile
dining car il vagone ristorante
dining room la sala da pranzo
dinner la cena; **have dinner** cenare
direct diretto
direction la direzione
directory enquiries informazioni elenco abbonati
dirty sporco
disabled invalido
disappear scomparire
disappointed deluso
disaster il disastro
disco la discoteca
disease la malattia
disgusting rivoltante
disinfectant il disinfettante
distance la distanza
distributor il distributore
district (*in town*) la zona

disturb disturbare
dive tuffarsi
divorced divorziato
do fare
doctor il dottore
document il documento
dog il cane
doll la bambola
donkey l'asino *m*
door la porta
double doppio
double room la camera doppia
down: I feel a bit down mi sento un po' giù; **down there** laggiù
downstairs di sotto
draught (*air*) la corrente
dream il sogno
dress il vestito
dress (*verb*) vestire; (*oneself*) vestirsi
dressing gown la vestaglia
drink (*noun*) la bibita
drink (*verb*) bere
drinking water l'acqua potabile *f*
drive guidare
driver l'autista *m*
driving licence la patente
drop la goccia
drop (*something*) far cadere
drug (*medical*) la medicina; (*narcotic*) la droga
drunk ubriaco
dry (*adjective*) asciutto
dry (*verb*) asciugare
dry-cleaner's il lavasecco
duck l'anatra *f*
durex (*R*) il preservativo
during durante
dustbin la pattumiera
Dutch olandese

duty-free esente da tasse
duty-free shop il duty free

each ciascuno
ear l'orecchio *m*
early presto; (*too early*) troppo presto
earrings gli orecchini
earth la terra
east l'est *m*; **east of** a est di
Easter Pasqua
easy facile
eat mangiare
eau de toilette l'acqua di Colonia *f*
egg l'uovo *m*; **boiled/ hard-boiled egg** uovo alla coque/ sodo
egg cup il portauovo
either ... or ... o ... o ...
elastic elastico
Elastoplast (R) il cerotto
elbow il gomito
electric elettrico
electricity l'elettricità *f*
else: something else qualcos'altro
elsewhere da qualche altra parte
embarrassing imbarazzante
embassy l'ambasciata *f*
emergency l'emergenza *f*
emergency exit l'uscita di sicurezza *f*
empty vuoto
end la fine
engaged (*toilet, phone*) occupato; (*to be married*) fidanzato

engine il motore; (*train*) la locomotiva
England l'Inghilterra *f*
English inglese
English girl/ woman l'inglese *f*
Englishman l'inglese *m*
enlargement (*photographic*) l'ingrandimento *m*
enough abbastanza; **that's enough** basta così
enter entrare in
entrance l'entrata *f*
envelope la busta
epileptic epilettico
especially specialmente
Eurocheque l'eurocheque *m*
Europe l'Europa *f*
European europeo
even: even men persino gli uomini; **even if** anche se; **even more beautiful** ancora più bello
evening la sera; **good evening** buonasera
every ogni; **every time** ogni volta
everyone ognuno
everything tutto
everywhere dappertutto
exaggerate esagerare
example l'esempio *m*; **for example** per esempio
excellent buonissimo
except eccetto
excess baggage il bagaglio in eccesso
exchange scambiare; **exchange rate** il tasso di cambio
exciting emozionante
excuse me permesso; (*for attention*) scusi

exhaust (*car*) il tubo di scappamento
exhibition la mostra
exit l'uscita *f*
expensive caro
explain spiegare
extension lead la prolunga
eye l'occhio *m*
eyebrow il sopracciglio
eyeliner l'eye-liner *m*
eye shadow l'ombretto *m*

face la faccia
factory la fabbrica
faint (*verb*) svenire
fair (*funfair*) il luna park
fair (*just*) giusto
fall cadere
false falso
family la famiglia
famous famoso
fan il ventilatore
fan belt la cinghia della ventola
far (away) lontano
farm la fattoria
farmer l'agricoltore *m*
fashion la moda
fashionable di moda
fast veloce
fat (*adjective*) grasso
fat (*noun*) il grasso
father il padre
father-in-law il suocero
fault: it's my/ his fault è colpa mia/ sua
faulty difettoso
favourite preferito
fear la paura

February febbraio
fed up: I'm fed up (with) sono stufo (di)
feel (*something*) sentire; **I feel well/ unwell** mi/ non mi sento bene; **I feel like ...** ho voglia di ...
feeling sensazione
felt-tip pen il pennarello
feminist femminista
fence lo steccato
ferry il traghetto
fever la febbre
few: few tourists pochi turisti; **a few children** qualche bambino
fiancé(e) il fidanzato, la fidanzata
field il campo
fight (*verb*) litigare
fight (*noun*) la lite
fill riempire
fillet il filetto
filling (*tooth*) l'otturazione *f*
film il film
filter il filtro
find trovare
fine (*adjective*) bello
fine (*noun*) la multa
finger il dito
fingernail l'unghia *f*
finish finire
fire il fuoco; (*blaze*) l'incendio *m*
fire brigade i vigili del fuoco
fire extinguisher l'estintore *m*
fireworks i fuochi d'artificio
first primo
first (*adverb*) per prima cosa
first aid il pronto soccorso
first class (*in train*) la prima classe

ENGLISH-ITALIAN

first floor il primo piano
first name il nome di
  battesimo
fish il pesce
fishbone la lisca
fishing la pesca
fishmonger's la pescheria
fit (*healthy*) in forma
fizzy frizzante
flag la bandiera
flash il flash
flat (*adj*) piatto; **a flat tyre**
  una gomma a terra
flat (*noun*) l'appartamento *m*
flavour il sapore
flea la pulce
flight il volo
flirt flirtare
floor (*of room*) il pavimento;
  (*storey*) il piano
florist il fioraio
flour la farina
flower il fiore
flu l'influenza *f*
fly (*insect*) la mosca
fly (*verb*) volare
fog la nebbia
folk music la musica folk
follow seguire
food il cibo
food poisoning
  l'intossicazione alimentare *f*
foot il piede; **on foot** a piedi
football il calcio
for per
forbidden vietato
forehead la fronte
foreign straniero
foreigner lo straniero
forest la foresta
forget dimenticare
fork (*for eating*) la forchetta;
  (*in road*) il bivio

form (*to fill in*) il modulo
fortnight: a fortnight
  quindici giorni
fortunately fortunatamente
forward (*mail*) inoltrare
foundation cream il fondo
  tinta
fountain la fontana
fracture la frattura
France la Francia
free libero; (*of charge*)
  gratuito
freezer il freezer
French francese
fresh fresco
Friday venerdì
fridge il frigo
friend l'amico *m*, l'amica *f*
from da
front il davanti; **in front of**
  davanti a
frost il gelo
frozen (*food*) surgelato
fruit la frutta
fry friggere
frying pan la padella
full pieno
full board la pensione
  completa
fun: have fun divertirsi
funeral il funerale
funnel (*pouring*) l'imbuto *m*
funny (*amusing*) buffo;
  (*strange*) strano
furious furioso
furniture i mobili
further più avanti
fuse il fusibile
future il futuro

G

game (*to play*) il gioco; (*meat*) la selvaggina
garage il garage
garden il giardino
garlic l'aglio *m*
gas il gas
gas permeable lenses le lenti semi-rigide
gauge (*petrol*) la spia
gay gay
gear il cambio
gearbox la scatola del cambio
gear lever la leva del cambio
gentleman il signore
gents (*toilet*) la toilette
genuine autentico
German tedesco
Germany la Germania
get prendere; **how do I get to ...?** come si arriva a ...?
get across attraversare
get back (*return*) tornare
get in (*car*) salire
get off scendere
get out! fuori!
get up alzarsi
gin il gin
gin and tonic il gin e tonica
girl la ragazza
girlfriend la ragazza
give dare
give back restituire
glad contento
glass il vetro; (*drinking*) il bicchiere
glasses gli occhiali
gloves i guanti
glue la colla
go andare

go away! vattene!
go down scendere
go in entrare
go out uscire
go through attraversare
go up salire
goat la capra
God Dio *m*
gold l'oro *m*
golf il golf
good buono; **good!** bene!
goodbye arrivederci
goose l'oca *f*
got: have you got ...? ha ...?
government il governo
grammar la grammatica
grandfather il nonno
grandmother la nonna
grapefruit il pompelmo
grapes l'uva *f*
grass l'erba *f*
grateful grato
greasy (*food*) grasso
great (*very good*) stupendo
Greece la Grecia
Greek greco
green verde
greengrocer il fruttivendolo
grey grigio
grilled alla griglia
grocer's il negozio di alimentari
ground floor il piano terra
group il gruppo
guarantee la garanzia
guest l'ospite *m/f*
guesthouse la pensione
guide la guida
guidebook la guida
guitar la chitarra
gun (*rifle*) il fucile

ENGLISH-ITALIAN

H

habit l'abitudine f
hail la grandine
hair i capelli
haircut il taglio di capelli
hairdresser's il parrucchiere
hair dryer il föhn
hair spray la lacca per capelli
half la metà; **half a litre/
  day** mezzo litro/ giorno;
  half an hour mezz'ora
half board la mezza pensione
ham il prosciutto
hamburger l'hamburger f
hammer il martello
hand la mano
handbag la borsetta
handbrake il freno a mano
handkerchief il fazzoletto
handle la maniglia
hand luggage il bagaglio a
  mano
handsome attraente
hanger la gruccia
hangover i postumi della
  sbornia
happen succedere
happy felice
harbour il porto
hard duro
hard lenses le lenti rigide
hat il cappello
hate detestare
have avere (see grammar); **I
  have to ...** devo ...
hay fever la febbre da fieno
hazelnut la nocciola
he lui (see grammar)
head la testa
headache il mal di testa

headlights i fari
health la salute
healthy sano
hear sentire
hearing aid l'apparecchio
  acustico m
heart il cuore
heart attack l'infarto m
heat il caldo
heater (in room) il radiatore
heating il riscaldamento
heavy pesante
heel (foot, shoe) il tallone
helicopter l'elicottero m
hello ciao!
help (verb) aiutare
help l'aiuto m; **help!** aiuto!
her (pronoun) la; **for her** per
  lei; **her boyfriend/
  girlfriend** il suo amico/ la
  sua amica (see grammar)
here qui; **here is/ are** ecco
hers il suo, la sua (see
  grammar)
hiccups il singhiozzo
hide (something) nascondere
high alto
highway code il codice
  stradale
hill la collina
him lo; **for him** per lui (see
  grammar)
hip il fianco
hire: **for hire** a nolo
his: **his boyfriend/ girlfriend**
  il suo amico/ la sua amica
  (see grammar)
history la storia
hit colpire
hitchhike fare l'autostop
hitchhiking l'autostop m
hobby l'hobby m
hold tenere

ENGLISH-ITALIAN

hole il buco
holiday la vacanza; *(public)* la festa; **the summer holidays** le vacanze estive
Holland l'Olanda *f*
home: at home a casa; **go home** andare a casa
homemade fatto in casa
homesick: I'm homesick ho nostalgia di casa
honest onesto
honey il miele
honeymoon la luna di miele
hoover *(R)* l'aspirapolvere *m*
hope sperare
horn il clacson
horrible orribile
horse il cavallo
horse riding l'equitazione *f*
hospital l'ospedale *m*
hospitality l'ospitalità *f*
hot caldo; *(to taste)* piccante
hotel l'albergo *m*
hot-water bottle la borsa dell'acqua calda
hour l'ora *f*
house la casa
house wine il vino della casa
how? come?; **how are things?** come va?
how many? quanti?
how much? quanto?
humour l'umorismo *m*
hungry: I'm hungry ho fame
hurry *(verb)* sbrigarsi
hurry up! sbrigati!
hurt far male
husband il marito

I io
ice il ghiaccio
ice cream il gelato
ice lolly il ghiacciolo
idea l'idea *f*
idiot l'idiota *m/f*
if se
ignition l'accensione *m*
ill malato
immediately immediatamente
important importante
impossible impossibile
improve migliorare
in in; **in Rimini** a Rimini; **in Italy/ Italian** in Italia/ italiano; **in 1945** nel 1945; **is he in?** c'è? *(see grammar)*
included compreso
incredible incredibile
independent indipendente
indicator *(car)* la freccia
indigestion l'indigestione *f*
industry l'industria *f*
infection l'infezione *f*
information l'informazione *f*
information desk il banco delle informazioni
injection l'iniezione *f*
injured ferito
inner tube la camera d'aria
innocent innocente
insect l'insetto *m*
insect repellent l'insettifugo *m*
inside dentro
insomnia l'insonnia *f*
instant coffee il caffè solubile
instructor il maestro

insurance l'assicurazione f
intelligent intelligente
interesting interessante
introduce presentare
invitation l'invito m
invite invitare
Ireland l'Irlanda f
Irish irlandese
iron (*metal*) il ferro; (*for clothes*) il ferro da stiro
iron (*verb*) stirare
ironmonger's il negozio di ferramenta
island l'isola f
it: it is è
Italian italiano
Italian girl/ woman l'italiana f
Italy l'Italia f
itch il prurito
IUD il contraccettivo intrauterino

jack (*car*) il cric
jacket la giacca
jam la marmellata
January gennaio
jaw la mascella
jazz il jazz
jealous geloso
jeans i jeans
jellyfish la medusa
jeweller's la gioielleria
jewellery i gioielli
Jewish ebreo
job l'impiego m
jogging: I go jogging faccio footing
joint (*to smoke*) lo spinello

joke lo scherzo
journey il viaggio; **have a good journey!** buon viaggio!
jug la brocca
juice il succo
July luglio
jump saltare
jumper il maglione
junction il bivio
June giugno
just: just two soltanto due

keep tenere
key la chiave
kidney il rene; (*to eat*) il rognone
kill uccidere
kilo il chilo
kilometre il chilometro
kind gentile
king il re
kiss (*verb*) baciare
kiss il bacio
kitchen la cucina
knee il ginocchio
knife il coltello
knit lavorare a maglia
knock over investire
know sapere; (*person*) conoscere; **I don't know** non lo so

label l'etichetta f
ladder la scala a pioli

ENGLISH-ITALIAN

ladies (*toilet*) la toilette
lady la signora
lager la birra chiara
lake il lago
lamb l'agnello *m*
lamp la lampada
land (*verb*) atterrare
landscape il paesaggio
language la lingua
language school la scuola di lingue
large grande
last ultimo; **last year** l'anno scorso; **at last** finalmente
late tardi; **I'm late** sono in ritardo; **later** più tardi
laugh ridere
launderette la lavanderia automatica
laundry (*dirty*) il bucato
law la legge
lawn il prato all'inglese
lawyer l'avvocato *m*
laxative il lassativo
lazy pigro
leaf la foglia
leaflet il dépliant
leak la perdita
learn imparare
least: at least come minimo
leather il cuoio; (*fine*) la pelle
leave (*go away*) partire; (*behind*) lasciare
left la sinistra; **on the left (of)** a sinistra (di)
left-handed mancino
left luggage il deposito bagagli
leg la gamba
lemon il limone
lemonade la limonata
lend prestare

length la lunghezza
lens l'obiettivo *m*
less meno
lesson la lezione
let (*allow*) permettere
letter la lettera
letterbox la buca delle lettere
lettuce la lattuga
level crossing il passaggio a livello
library la biblioteca
licence il permesso; (*driving*) la patente
lid il coperchio
lie (*say untruth*) mentire
lie down stendersi
life la vita
lift l'ascensore *m*; **give a lift** dare un passaggio a
light (*in room*) la luce; **light** (*on car*) il faro; **have you got a light?** può farmi accendere?
light (*verb*) accendere
light (*adjective*) leggero; **light blue** blu chiaro
light bulb la lampadina
lighter l'accendino *m*
lighthouse il faro
light meter l'esposimetro *m*
like: I like cheese/ eating mi piace il formaggio/ mangiare; **I would like** vorrei
like (*as*) come
lip il labbro
lipstick il rossetto
liqueur il liquore
list la lista
listen (to) ascoltare
litre il litro
litter i rifiuti

ENGLISH-ITALIAN

little piccolo; **a little** un
  po'; **a little bit of** un po' di
live vivere; (*in place*) abitare
liver il fegato
living room la sala
lizard la lucertola
lobster l'aragosta *f*
lock (*verb*) chiudere a chiave
lock (*noun*) la serratura
lollipop il lecca lecca
London Londra
long lungo; **a long time**
  tanto tempo
look (at) guardare; (*seem*)
  avere l'aria
look for cercare
look like (*resemble*)
  assomigliare a
look out! attenzione!
lorry il camion
lose perdere
lost property office l'ufficio
  oggetti smarriti *m*
lot: **a lot** molto; **a lot of wine/**
  men molto vino/ molti
  uomini
loud forte
lounge il soggiorno
love (*verb*) amare
love l'amore *m*; **make love**
  fare l'amore
lovely delizioso
low basso
luck la fortuna; **good luck!**
  buona fortuna!
luggage bagagli *mpl*
lukewarm tiepido
lunch il pranzo
lungs i polmoni

macho macho
mad pazzo
Madam signora
magazine la rivista
maiden name il nome da
  ragazza
mail la posta
main principale
make fare
make-up il trucco
male chauvinist pig lo sporco
  maschilista
man l'uomo *m*
manager il direttore
many: **many people/**
  countries molte persone/
  molti paesi
map la cartina; (*of town*) la
  pianta
March marzo
margarine la margarina
market il mercato
marmalade la marmellata
  d'arance
married sposato
mascara il mascara
mass la messa
match il fiammifero
match (*sport*) l'incontro *m*
material la stoffa
matter: **it doesn't matter** non
  importa
mattress il materasso
May maggio
maybe forse
mayonnaise la maionese
me mi; **for me** per me; **it's**
  me sono io (*see grammar*)
meal il pasto; **enjoy your**

meal! buon appetito!
mean (*verb*) significare
measles il morbillo; **German measles** la rosolia
meat la carne
mechanic il meccanico
medicine la medicina
medieval medievale
Mediterranean il Mediterraneo
medium (*steak*) non troppo cotta
meet incontrarsi; (*someone*) incontrare
meeting la riunione
melon il melone
mend riparare
menu il menù; **set menu** il menù fisso
mess il pasticcio
message il messaggio
metal il metallo
metre il metro
midday mezzogiorno
middle il mezzo
Middle Ages il Medio Evo
midnight mezzanotte
milk il latte
minced meat la carne macinata
mind: do you mind if ...? le dispiace se ...?
mine il mio, la mia (*see grammar*)
mineral water l'acqua minerale *f*
minute il minuto
mirror lo specchio
Miss signorina
miss (*train etc*) perdere; **I miss you** mi manchi
mistake lo sbaglio
misunderstanding

l'equivoco *m*
mix mischiare
modern moderno
moisturizer il prodotto idratante
Monday lunedì
money i soldi
month il mese
monument il monumento
mood l'umore *m*
moon la luna
moped il motorino
more più; **more than** più di; **... no more ... ** più
morning la mattina; **good morning** buongiorno
mosquito la zanzara
most (of) la maggior parte (di)
mother la madre
mother-in-law la suocera
motorbike la motocicletta
motorboat il motoscafo
motorway l'autostrada *f*
mountain la montagna
mouse il topo
moustache i baffi
mouth la bocca
Mr signor
Mrs signora
Ms signora, signorina
much molto
mum la mamma
muscle il muscolo
museum il museo
mushrooms i funghi
music la musica
musical instrument lo strumento musicale
mussels le cozze
must: I/ you/ he must devo/ devi/ deve
mustard la senape

my il mio, la mia (*see grammar*)

nail (*in wall*) il chiodo; (*on finger*) l'unghia *f*
nail clippers il tagliaunghie
nailfile la lima per le unghie
nail polish lo smalto per le unghie
nail polish remover l'acetone *m*
naked nudo
name il nome; **my name is Jim** mi chiamo Jim
napkin il tovagliolo
nappy il pannolino; **disposable nappies** pannolini da buttare
nappy-liners i proteggi-pannolino
narrow stretto
nationality la nazionalità
natural naturale
nature la natura
near vicino a; **near here** qui vicino; **nearest** più vicino
nearly quasi
necessary necessario
neck il collo
necklace la collana
need: I need . . . ho bisogno di . . .
needle l'ago *m*
negative (*film*) la negativa
neighbour il vicino
neither . . . nor . . . né . . . né . . .
nephew il nipote
nervous nervoso

neurotic nevrotico
never mai
new nuovo
news le notizie
newsagent il giornalaio
newspaper il giornale
New Year l'anno nuovo *m*; **Happy New Year** Buon Anno
next prossimo; **next year** l'anno prossimo
next to vicino a
nice (*person*) simpatico; (*meal*) buono; (*to look at*) bello
nickname il soprannome
niece la nipote
night la notte; **good night** buona notte
nightclub il night
nightdress la camicia da notte
nightmare l'incubo *m*
no (*reply*) no; **there is no soap** non c'è sapone; **there is no more water** non c'è più acqua; **no longer** non più
nobody nessuno
noise il rumore
noisy rumoroso
non-smoking non fumatori
normal normale
north il nord; **north of** a nord di
Northern Ireland l'Irlanda del Nord *f*
nose il naso
not non; **I'm not tired** non sono stanco
notebook il taccuino
nothing niente
novel il romanzo

ENGLISH-ITALIAN

November novembre
now adesso
nowhere da nessuna parte
number il numero
number plate la targa
nurse l'infermiera *f*
nut (to eat) la noce; (for bolt)
il dado

obnoxious detestabile
obvious ovvio
October ottobre
octopus il polipo
of di (see grammar)
off (lights) spento
offend offendere
offer (verb) offrire
office l'ufficio *m*
often spesso
oil l'olio *m*
ointment l'unguento *m*
OK d'accordo; I'm OK sto
bene
old vecchio; how old are
you? quanti anni hai?; I'm
25 years old ho 25 anni
old-age pensioner il
pensionato, la pensionata
olive l'oliva *f*
olive oil l'olio d'oliva *m*
omelette l'omelette *f*
on su; (lights) acceso
once una volta
one uno, *f* una
onion la cipolla
only solo
open (adjective) aperto
open (verb) aprire
opera l'opera *f*

operation l'operazione *f*
opposite di fronte a
optician l'ottico *m*
optimistic ottimista
or o
orange (fruit) l'arancia *f*
orange (colour) arancione
orchestra l'orchestra *f*
order (meal) ordinare
organize organizzare
other altro
otherwise altrimenti
our, ours il nostro, la nostra
(see grammar)
out: she's out è fuori
outside fuori
oven il forno
over (above) su; (finished)
finito; over there laggiù
overdone troppo cotto
overtake sorpassare
owner il proprietario
oyster l'ostrica *f*

pack (luggage) fare le valigie
package il pacco
package tour la gita
organizzata
packed lunch la colazione al
sacco
packet (of cigarettes etc) il
pacchetto
page la pagina
pain il dolore
painful doloroso
painkiller l'analgesico *m*
paint (verb) dipingere
paint brush il pennello
painting il dipinto

75

pair il paio
palace il palazzo
pancake la crêpe
panic il panico
panties le mutandine
paper la carta
parcel il pacco
pardon? prego?
parents i genitori
park (garden) il parco
park (car) parcheggiare
part la parte
party (celebration) la festa; (group) il gruppo
pass (mountain) il passo
passenger il passeggero
passport il passaporto
pasta la pasta
pâté il pâté
path il sentiero
pavement il marciapiede
pay pagare
peach la pesca
peanuts le noccioline americane
pear la pera
peas i piselli
pedal il pedale
pedestrian il pedone
pedestrian crossing l'attraversamento pedonale m
pedestrian precinct la zona pedonale
pen la penna
pencil la matita
pencil sharpener il temperamatite
penicillin la penicillina
penis il pene
penknife il temperino
people la gente
pepper (spice) il pepe; (vegetable) il peperone

per: per week per settimana
per cent per cento
perfect perfetto
perfume il profumo
period il periodo; (woman's) le mestruazioni
perm la permanente
person la persona
petrol la benzina
petrol station la stazione di servizio
phone (verb) telefonare (a)
phone book la guida telefonica
phone box la cabina telefonica
phone number il numero di telefono
photograph la fotografia
photograph (verb) fotografare
photographer il fotografo
phrase book il frasario
pickpocket il borsaiolo
picnic il picnic
pie (fruit) la torta
piece il pezzo
pig il maiale
piles le emorroidi
pill la pillola
pillow il cuscino
pilot il pilota
pin lo spillo
pineapple l'ananas m
pink rosa
pipe (tube) il tubo; (to smoke) la pipa
pity: it's a pity è un peccato
pizza la pizza
plane l'aereo m
plant la pianta
plastic la plastica; plastic bag il sacchetto di plastica

76

plate il piatto
platform il binario
play (*verb*) giocare
pleasant piacevole
please per favore
pleased contento; **pleased to meet you** piacere di conoscerla
pliers le pinze
plug (*electrical*) la spina; (*in sink*) il tappo
plum la prugna
plumber l'idraulico *m*
p.m.: at 3/11p.m. alle 3 del pomeriggio/ 11 di sera
pneumonia la polmonite
pocket la tasca
poison il veleno
police la polizia
policeman il poliziotto
police station la stazione di polizia
polite educato
political politico
politics la politica
polluted inquinato
pond lo stagno
poor povero
pop music la musica pop
pork il maiale
port (*drink*) il porto
porter (*hotel*) il portiere
possible possibile
post (*verb*) impostare
postcard la cartolina
poster (*for room*) il poster; (*in street*) il manifesto
poste restante il fermo posta
postman il postino
post office l'ufficio postale *m*
potato la patata
poultry il pollame
pound (*weight*) la libbra;

(*sterling*) la sterlina
power cut l'interruzione della corrente *f*
practical pratico
pram la carrozzina
prawn il gambero
prefer preferire
pregnant incinta
prepare preparare
prescription la ricetta medica
present (*gift*) il regalo
pretty grazioso
price il prezzo
priest il prete
prince il principe
princess la principessa
printed matter lo stampato
prison la prigione
private privato
probably probabilmente
problem il problema
programme il programma
prohibited proibito
promise (*verb*) promettere
pronounce pronunciare
protect proteggere
Protestant protestante
proud fiero
public pubblico
pull tirare
pump (*for bike etc*) la pompa
puncture la foratura
punk punk
purple viola
purse il borsellino
push spingere
pushchair il passeggino
put mettere
pyjamas il pigiama

ENGLISH-ITALIAN

quality la qualità
quarter il quarto
quay il molo
queen la regina
question la domanda
queue la fila
queue (*verb*) fare la fila
quick veloce
quickly velocemente
quiet tranquillo; **quiet!** silenzio!
quilt la trapunta
quite abbastanza; **quite a lot** parecchio

rabbit il coniglio
radiator il radiatore
radio la radio
railway la ferrovia
rain la pioggia
rain (*verb*) piovere; **it's raining** piove
rainbow l'arcobaleno *m*
raincoat l'impermeabile *m*
rape lo stupro
rare raro; (*steak*) al sangue
raspberry il lampone
rat il ratto
rather piuttosto
raw crudo
razor il rasoio
razor blade la lametta
read leggere
ready pronto

really veramente
rear lights i fari posteriori
rearview mirror lo specchietto retrovisore
receipt la ricevuta
receive ricevere
reception (*hotel*) la reception
receptionist il/ la receptionist
recipe la ricetta
recognize riconoscere
recommend consigliare
record il disco
record player il giradischi
record shop il negozio di dischi
red rosso
red-headed rosso di capelli
refund (*verb*) rimborsare
relax rilassarsi
religion la religione
remember ricordarsi di; **I remember** mi ricordo
rent (*house etc*) affittare; (*car*) noleggiare
rent (*price*) l'affitto *m*
repair riparare
repeat ripetere
reservation la prenotazione
reserve prenotare
responsible responsabile
rest (*remaining*) il resto; **take a rest** riposarsi
restaurant il ristorante
return ticket il biglietto di andata e ritorno
reverse (*gear*) la retromarcia
reverse charge call la telefonata a carico del destinatario
rheumatism il reumatismo
rib la costola
rice il riso
rich ricco; (*food*) sostanzioso

ridiculous ridicolo
right (*correct*) giusto
right (*side*) la destra; **on the right** (**of**) a destra (di)
right of way la precedenza
ring (*on finger*) l'anello *m*
ring (*someone*) telefonare (a)
ripe maturo
river il fiume
road la strada
roadsign il segnale stradale
roadworks i lavori stradali
rock la roccia
rock climbing la roccia
rock music il rock
roll il panino
roof il tetto
roof rack il portapacchi
room la stanza
rope la corda
rose la rosa
rosé wine il rosé
rotten marcio
round (*circular*) rotondo
route l'itinerario *m*
rowing boat la barca a remi
rubber la gomma
rubber band l'elastico *m*
rubbish i rifiuti
rucksack lo zaino
rude sgarbato
rug il tappeto
ruins le rovine
rum il rum
run correre

sad triste
safe sicuro
safety pin la spilla di

sicurezza
sailboard la tavola a vela
sailing la vela
sailing boat la barca a vela
salad l'insalata *f*
salad dressing il condimento per l'insalata
sale la vendita; (*reduced prices*) i saldi; **for sale** vendesi
salmon il salmone
salt il sale
salty salato
same stesso
sand la sabbia
sandals i sandali
sand dunes le dune
sandwich il panino imbottito
sanitary towel l'assorbente igienico *m*
sardine la sardina
Saturday sabato
sauce la salsa
saucepan la pentola
saucer il piattino
sauna la sauna
sausage la salsiccia
savoury salato
say dire
Scandinavia la Scandinavia
scarf la sciarpa
scenery il paesaggio
school la scuola
science la scienza
scissors le forbici
Scotland la Scozia
Scottish scozzese
scrambled eggs le uova strapazzate
scream strillare
screw la vite
screwdriver il cacciavite
sea il mare

seafood i frutti di mare
seagull il gabbiano
seasick: I'm seasick ho il mal di mare
seaside: at the seaside al mare
season la stagione; **in the high season** in alta stagione
seat il posto
seat belt la cintura di sicurezza
seaweed le alghe marine
second (*time*) il secondo
second-hand di seconda mano
secret segreto
see vedere; **see you tomorrow** a domani
self-service self-service
sell vendere
sellotape (R) lo scotch
send mandare
sensible sensato
sensitive sensibile
separate separato
separately separatamente
September settembre
serious serio
serve (*meal*) servire
service il servizio
service charge il prezzo del servizio
serviette il tovagliolo
several diversi
sew cucire
sex il sesso
sexist sessista
sexy sexy
shade l'ombra *f*
shampoo lo shampoo
share (*verb*) dividere
shark lo squalo
shave farsi la barba

shaving brush il pennello da barba
shaving foam la schiuma da barba
she lei (*see grammar*)
sheet il lenzuolo
shell la conchiglia
shellfish i frutti di mare
ship la nave
shirt la camicia
shock lo shock
shock-absorber l'ammortizzatore *m*
shocking scandaloso
shoe laces le stringhe
shoe polish il lucido per le scarpe
shoe repairer il calzolaio
shoes le scarpe
shop il negozio
shopping le compere; **go shopping** andare a fare le compere
shopping bag la borsa della spesa
shopping centre il centro commerciale
shore la sponda
short corto
shortcut la scorciatoia
shorts i calzoncini
shortsighted miope
shoulder la spalla
shout gridare
show (*verb*) far vedere
shower la doccia; (*rain*) l'acquazzone *m*
shutter (*photo*) l'otturatore *m*
shutters (*window*) le imposte
shy timido
sick: I feel sick ho la nausea; **I'm going to be sick** sto per vomitare

ENGLISH-ITALIAN

side il lato
sidelights le luci di posizione
sign (verb) firmare
silence il silenzio
silk la seta
silver l'argento m
silver foil la stagnola
similar simile
simple semplice
since (time) da quando
sincere sincero
sing cantare
single (man) celibe; (woman) nubile
single room la camera singola
single ticket il biglietto di andata
sink (in kitchen) l'acquaio m
sink (go under) affondare
sir signore
sister la sorella
sister-in-law la cognata
sit down sedersi
size la taglia
ski lo sci
ski (verb) sciare
ski boots gli scarponi da sci
skid scivolare
skiing lo sci
ski-lift lo ski-lift
skin la pelle
skin cleanser il latte detergente
skin-diving l'immersione f
skinny mingherlino
skirt la gonna
ski slope il campo da sci
skull il teschio; (of living person) il cranio
sky il cielo
sleep dormire
sleeper il vagone letto

sleeping bag il sacco a pelo
sleeping pill il sonnifero
sleepy: I'm sleepy ho sonno
slice la fetta
slide (photo) la diapositiva
slim snello
slippers le pantofole
slippery scivoloso
slow lento
slowly lentamente
small piccolo
smell (verb) sentire odore di
smell l'odore m
smile (verb) sorridere
smoke (verb) fumare
smoke il fumo
smoking (compartment) fumatori
snack lo spuntino
snake il serpente
sneeze starnutire
snore russare
snow la neve
so: so beautiful così bello
soaking solution la soluzione salina per lenti
soap il sapone
society la società
socket la presa
socks i calzini
soft morbido
soft drink la bibita analcolica
soft lenses le lenti morbide
sole (of shoe) la suola
some: some wine/ biscuits del vino/ dei biscotti (see grammar)
somebody qualcuno
something qualcosa
sometimes qualche volta
somewhere da qualche parte
son il figlio
song la canzone

son-in-law il genero
soon presto
sore: I've got a sore throat ho il mal di gola
sorry mi scusi
soup la minestra
sour aspro
south il sud; **south of** a sud di
souvenir il souvenir
spade la vanga
Spain la Spagna
Spanish spagnolo
spanner la chiave inglese
spare parts i pezzi di ricambio
spare tyre la gomma di scorta
spark plug la candela
speak parlare
speciality la specialità
speed la velocità
speed limit il limite di velocità
speedometer il tachimetro
spend spendere
spice la spezia
spider il ragno
spinach gli spinaci
spoke il raggio
spoon il cucchiaio
sport lo sport
spot (on skin) il foruncolo
sprain: I sprained my ankle mi sono slogato una caviglia
spring (season) la primavera; (in seat etc) la molla
square (in town) la piazza
stain la macchia
stairs le scale
stamp il francobollo
stand: I can't stand cheese detesto il formaggio
star la stella

starter (food) l'antipasto m
state lo stato
station la stazione
stationer's il cartolaio
statue la statua
stay (remain) fermarsi; (in hotel etc) alloggiare
stay la permanenza
steak la bistecca
steal rubare
steamer il battello
steep ripido
steering lo sterzo
steering wheel il volante
stepfather il patrigno
stepmother la matrigna
steward lo steward
stewardess la hostess
still (adverb) ancora
sting pungere
stockings le calze
stomach lo stomaco
stomach ache il mal di stomaco
stone la pietra
stop (verb) fermare; **stop!** fermo!; **stop it!** smettila!
stop la fermata
storm la tempesta
story la storia
straight ahead avanti diritto
strange (odd) strano
strawberry la fragola
stream il ruscello
street la strada
string lo spago
stroke (attack) il colpo
strong forte
stuck bloccato
student lo studente, la studentessa
stupid stupido
suburbs la periferia

ENGLISH-ITALIAN

success il successo
suddenly improvvisamente
suede la pelle scamosciata
sugar lo zucchero
suit: blue suits you il blu le
 sta bene
suit (*to wear*) il completo
suitcase la valigia
summer l'estate *f*
sun il sole
sunbathe prendere il sole
sunburn la scottatura
Sunday domenica
sunglasses gli occhiali da sole
sunny assolato
sunset il tramonto
sunshine la luce del sole
sunstroke il colpo di sole
suntan l'abbronzatura *f*
suntan lotion la lozione
 solare
suntan oil l'olio solare *m*
supermarket il supermercato
supplement il supplemento
sure sicuro
surf il surf
surname il cognome
surprise la sorpresa
surprising sorprendente
swallow ingoiare
sweat (*verb*) sudare
sweater il maglione
sweet (*adjective*) dolce
sweet (*candy*) la caramella
swim nuotare
swimming il nuoto; **go
 swimming** andare a
 nuotare
swimming costume il
 costume da bagno
swimming pool la piscina
swimming trunks il costume
 da bagno

Swiss svizzero
switch (*noun*) l'interruttore *m*
switch off spegnere
switch on accendere
Switzerland la Svizzera
swollen gonfio
synagogue la sinagoga

table il tavolo
tablecloth la tovaglia
tablet (*drug*) la compressa
table tennis il ping-pong
tail la coda
take prendere
take away (*remove*) togliere;
 to take away (*food*) da
 portar via
take off (*plane*) decollare
talcum powder il talco
talk parlare
tall alto
tampon il tampone
tan l'abbronzatura *f*
tank il serbatoio
tap il rubinetto
tape (*cassette*) il nastro
tart la torta
taste (*noun*) il gusto
taste (*try*) assaggiare
taxi il taxi
tea il tè
teach insegnare
teacher l'insegnante *m/f*
team la squadra
teapot la teiera
tea towel lo strofinaccio
teenager l'adolescente *m/f*
telegram il telegramma
telephone il telefono

83

telephone directory la guida del telefono
television la televisione
temperature la temperatura
tennis il tennis
tent la tenda
terrible terribile
than: uglier than più brutto di
thank ringraziare
thank you grazie
that (*adjective*) quello, quella; (*pronoun*) quello; **that one** quello lì; **I think that ...** penso che ...
the il, lo, la; (*plural*) i, gli, le (*see grammar*)
theatre il teatro
their, theirs il/ la loro (*see grammar*)
them li; **for them** per loro (*see grammar*)
then allora
there là; **there is** c'è; **there are** ci sono
thermometer il termometro
thermos flask il thermos
these questi, queste
they loro (*see grammar*)
thick spesso
thief il ladro
thigh la coscia
thin sottile
thing la cosa
think pensare
thirsty: I'm thirsty ho sete
this (*adjective*) questo, questa; (*pronoun*) questo; **this one** questo qui
those questi, queste
thread il filo
throat la gola
throat pastilles le pastiglie per la gola
through attraverso
throw gettare
throw away buttare via
thunder il tuono
thunderstorm il temporale
Thursday giovedì
ticket il biglietto
ticket office la biglietteria
tide la marea
tie (*to wear*) la cravatta
tight attillato
tights il collant
time il tempo; (*occasion*) la volta; **what time is it?** che ore sono?; **on time** (*person*) puntuale
timetable l'orario *m*
tin opener l'apriscatole *m*
tip (*to waiter etc*) la mancia
tired stanco
tissues i fazzolettini di carta
to: I'm going to Parma/ Scotland vado a Parma/ in Scozia
toast (*bread*) il pane tostato
tobacco il tabacco
today oggi
toe il dito del piede
together insieme
toilet la toilette
toilet paper la carta igienica
tomato il pomodoro
tomorrow domani
tongue la lingua
tonight stanotte
tonsillitis la tonsillite
too: too big troppo grande; **not too much** non troppo; **me too** anche io
tool l'utensile *m*
tooth il dente
toothache il mal di denti

ENGLISH-ITALIAN

toothbrush lo spazzolino da denti
toothpaste il dentifricio
top: at the top in cima
torch la torcia elettrica
touch toccare
tourist il/la turista
towel l'asciugamano *m*
tower la torre
town la città
toy il giocattolo
tracksuit la tuta da ginnastica
tradition la tradizione
traditional tradizionale
traffic il traffico
traffic jam l'ingorgo *m*
traffic lights il semaforo
traffic warden il vigile urbano
trailer (*behind car*) il rimorchio
train il treno
trainers le scarpe da ginnastica
translate tradurre
transmission la trasmissione
travel viaggiare
travel agent's l'agenzia di viaggio *f*
traveller's cheque il travellers' chèque
tray il vassoio
tree l'albero *m*
trip la gita
trolley il carrello
trousers i pantaloni
true vero
try provare
try on provare
T-shirt la maglietta
Tuesday martedì
tuna fish il tonno
tunnel il tunnel
turkey il tacchino

turn girare
tweezers le pinzette
twins i gemelli
typewriter la macchina da scrivere
tyre il pneumatico

ugly brutto
umbrella l'ombrello *m*
uncle lo zio
under sotto
underdone poco cotto
underground la metropolitana
underpants le mutande
understand capire
underwear la biancheria intima
unemployed disoccupato
unfortunately sfortunatamente
United States gli Stati Uniti
university l'università *f*
unpack disfare le valigie
unpleasant sgradevole
until finché
up: up there lassù
upstairs di sopra
urgent urgente
us ci; **for us** per noi (*see grammar*)
use usare
useful utile
usual solito
usually di solito

ENGLISH-ITALIAN

V

vaccination la vaccinazione
vacuum cleaner
  l'aspirapolvere *m*
vagina la vagina
valid valido
valley la valle
valve la valvola
van il furgone
vanilla la vaniglia
vase il vaso
VD la malattia venerea
veal il vitello
vegetables la verdura
vegetarian vegetariano
vehicle il veicolo
very molto; very much
  moltissimo
vet il veterinario
video il video
video recorder il
  videoregistratore
view la vista
viewfinder il mirino
villa la villa
village il villaggio
vinegar l'aceto *m*
vineyard la vigna
visa il visto
visit la visita
visit (*verb*) visitare
vitamins le vitamine
voice la voce

W

waist la vita
wait aspettare; wait for me!
aspettami!
waiter il cameriere
waiting room la sala d'attesa
waitress la cameriera
wake (*someone*) svegliare
wake up (*oneself*) svegliarsi
Wales il Galles
walk (*verb*) camminare
walk la passeggiata; go for a
  walk andare a fare una
  passeggiata
walkman (R) il walkman (R)
wall il muro
wallet il portafoglio
want volere; I want ...
  voglio ...; do you
  want ...? vuole ...?
war la guerra
warm caldo; it's warm fa
  caldo
wash lavare; (*oneself*) lavarsi
washbasin il lavabo
washing il bucato
washing machine la lavatrice
washing powder il detersivo
  per bucato
washing-up: do the washing-
  up lavare i piatti
washing-up liquid il
  detersivo liquido per i piatti
wasp la vespa
watch l'orologio *m*
watch (*verb*) guardare
water l'acqua *f*
waterfall la cascata
waterski lo sci acquatico
wave l'onda *f*
way: this way (*like this*) così;
  can you tell me the way to
  ...? mi può indicare la
  strada per ...?
we noi (*see grammar*)
weak debole

86

ENGLISH-ITALIAN

weather il tempo; **the
  weather is good** fa un
  tempo splendido
weather forecast le previsioni
  del tempo
wedding il matrimonio
Wednesday mercoledì
week la settimana
weekend il fine settimana
weight il peso
welcome! benvenuto!
well bene; **she's well/ not
  well** sta/ non sta bene
well done ben cotto
wellingtons gli stivali di
  gomma
Welsh gallese
west l'ovest *m*; **west of** a
  ovest di
wet umido
what? che cosa?
wheel la ruota
wheelchair la sedia a rotelle
when quando
where dove
which quale
while mentre
whipped cream la panna
  montata
whisky il whisky
white bianco
who? chi?; **the person who**
  la persona che
whole intero
whooping cough la pertosse
whose: **whose is this?** di chi è
  questo?
why perché
wide largo
widow la vedova
widower il vedovo
wife la moglie
wild (*animal*) . selvaggio

win vincere
wind il vento
window la finestra
windscreen il parabrezza
windscreen wiper il
  tergicristallo
wine il vino; **red/ white
  wine** il vino rosso/ bianco
wine list la lista dei vini
wing l'ala *f*
winter l'inverno *m*
wire il filo di ferro
wish: **best wishes** tanti
  auguri
with con
without senza
witness il testimone
woman la donna
wonderful meraviglioso
wood il legno
wool la lana
word la parola
work il lavoro
work (*verb*) lavorare; **it's not
  working** non funziona
world il mondo
worry la preoccupazione
worry about preoccuparsi
  per
worse peggio
worst peggiore
wound la ferita
wrap incartare
wrapping paper la carta da
  pacchi
wrench (*tool*) la chiave
  inglese
wrist il polso
write scrivere
writing paper la carta da
  lettere
wrong sbagliato

ENGLISH-ITALIAN

X-ray i raggi X

yacht lo yacht
year l'anno m
yellow giallo
yes sì
yesterday ieri
yet: not yet non ancora
yoghurt lo yogurt
you lei; (*familiar*) tu; **I know
   you** la/ti conosco; **for you**
   per lei/te (*see grammar*)
young giovane
young people i giovani
your, yours il suo, la sua;
   (*familiar*) il tuo, la tua (*see
   grammar*)
youth hostel l'ostello della
   gioventù m

zero zero
zip la cerniera lampo
zoo lo zoo

A

a: alla stazione at the station; **a Londra** in London; **vado a Londra** I'm going to London; **alle tre** at 3 o'clock; **a domani** see you tomorrow; **alla settimana** per week
abbastanza enough; quite
abbronzatura f suntan
abitare live
abiti mpl clothes
abito m dress; suit
abitudine f habit
acceleratore m accelerator
accendere switch on; light; **mi fa' accendere?** have you got a light?
accendino m lighter
accensione f ignition
accento m accent
accettare accept
accompagnare accompany
accordo m: **d'accordo** all right
aceto m vinegar
acetone m nail polish remover
acqua f water; **acqua potabile** drinking water
acqua di Colonia f eau de toilette
acquaio m sink
acqua minerale f mineral water

addormentato asleep
adesso now
adolescente m teenager
adulto m adult
aeroplano m aeroplane
aeroporto m airport
affari mpl business
affittare rent
affitto m rent
affollato crowded
affondare sink
agenzia f agency
agenzia di viaggio f travel agent's
aggiustare mend
aggressivo aggressive
agli at the; to the (see grammar)
aglio m garlic
agnello m lamb
ago m needle
agosto August
agricoltore m farmer
ai at the; to the (see grammar)
aids m AIDS
aiutare help
aiuto m help
al at the; to the (see grammar)
ala f wing
albergo m hotel
albero m tree
albero a gomiti m crankshaft
albicocca f apricot
alcool m alcohol
alghe marine fpl seaweed
alla at the; to the (see grammar)
allarme m alarm

allattare breastfeed
alle at the; to the (*see grammar*)
allergico a allergic to
allo at the; to the (*see grammar*)
alloggiare stay
alloggio *m* accommodation
allora then
almeno at least
alternatore *m* alternator
alto high; tall; **alto 2 metri** 2 m high
altrimenti otherwise
altro other; **un altro** another
alzarsi get up
amare love
amaro bitter
ambasciata *f* embassy
ambulanza *f* ambulance
America *f* America
americano American
amico *m*, **amica** *f* friend
ammobiliato furnished
ammortizzatore *m* shock-absorber
amore *m* love; **fare l'amore** make love
ampère: da 15 ampère 15-amp
analgesico *m* painkiller
ananas *m* pineapple
anatra *f* duck
anche also; even; **anche io** me too
ancora still; **ancora una birra** another beer; **ancora più bello** even more beautiful; **non ancora** not yet
ancora *f* anchor
andare go; **andiamo!** let's go!

anello *m* ring
angolo *m* corner
animale *m* animal
anniversario di matrimonio *m* wedding anniversary
anno *m* year
anno nuovo *m* New Year
annullare cancel
antenato *m* ancestor
antenna *f* aerial
antibiotico *m* antibiotic
anticipo: in anticipo in advance; early
antico ancient
antigelo *m* antifreeze
antipasto *m* starter
antiquariato *m*: **è un pezzo d'antiquariato** it's an antique; **un negozio di antiquariato** an antique shop
antisettico antiseptic
antistaminico *m* antihistamine
ape *f* bee
aperitivo *m* aperitif
aperto open
apparecchio acustico *m* hearing aid
appartamento *m* flat
appendicite *f* appendicitis
appetito *m* appetite; **buon appetito!** enjoy your meal!
appuntamento *m* appointment
aprile April
aprire open
apriscatole *m* tin opener
arachidi *fpl* peanuts
aragosta *f* lobster
arancia *f* orange
archeologia *f* archaeology

arcobaleno m rainbow
argento m silver
aria f air; **avere l'aria** look
aria condizionata f air-
  conditioning
armadio m cupboard
arrabbiato angry
arrestare arrest
arrivare arrive
arrivederci goodbye
arrivo m arrival
arte f art
artificiale artificial
artigianato m crafts
artista m artist
ascensore m lift
ascia f axe
asciugamano m towel
asciugare dry
asciugatura con föhn f blow-
  dry
asciutto dry
ascoltare listen
asino m donkey
asma f asthma
asparagi mpl asparagus
aspettare wait
aspirapolvere m hoover (R)
aspirina f aspirin
aspro sour
assaggiare taste
assegno m cheque
assicurazione f insurance
associazione f society
assolato sunny
assorbente igienico m
  sanitary towel
Atlantico m Atlantic
attaccato stuck
attento careful
attenzione! look out!
atterrare land
attillato tight

attraente attractive
attraversamento m
  pedestrian crossing
attraversare go through
attraverso through
auguri mpl: **tanti auguri** best
  wishes
aumentare increase
Austria f Austria
austriaco Austrian
autentico genuine
autista m driver
auto f car
autobus m bus
automatico automatic
automobilista m car driver
autostop m hitchhiking; **fare
  l'autostop** hitchhike
autostrada f motorway
autunno m autumn
avanti: avanti! come in!;
  avanti diritto straight
  ahead; **più avanti** further
avere have (see grammar)
avvicinarsi approach
avviso m notice
avvocato m lawyer
azzurro blue

baby-sitter m/f baby-sitter
bacio m kiss
baffi mpl moustache
bagagli mpl luggage
bagagliaio m boot
bagaglio m: **bagaglio a mano**
  hand luggage; **bagaglio in
  eccesso** excess baggage
bagnato wet
bagno m bath; bathroom

balcone *m* balcony
ballare dance
bambino *m* child
bambola *f* doll
banana *f* banana
banca *f* bank
banco informazioni *m* information desk
banconota *f* banknote
bandiera *f* flag
bar *m* bar; café
barba *f* beard; **farsi la barba** shave
barbiere *m* barber
barca a remi *f* rowing boat
barca a vela *f* sailing boat
basso low
basta: basta così that's enough
battello *m* steamer
batteria *f* battery
bebè *m/f* baby
beige beige
belga Belgian
Belgio *m* Belgium
bello beautiful
bene well; good
benissimo! excellent!
benvenuto! welcome!
benzina *f* petrol
bere drink
berretto *m* cap
biancheria da letto *f* bed linen
biancheria intima *f* underwear
bianco white
bianco e nero black and white
bibita *f* drink
bibita analcolica *f* soft drink
biblioteca *f* library
bicchiere *m* glass

bicicletta *f* bicycle
bigliettaio *m* conductor
biglietteria *f* ticket office
biglietto *m* ticket; **biglietto di andata** single ticket; **biglietto di andata e ritorno** return ticket
biglietto da visita *m* card
binario *m* platform
biondo blond
biro *f* biro (R)
birra *f* beer
birra chiara *f* lager
biscotto *m* biscuit
bisogno: ho bisogno di I need
bistecca *f* steak
bivio *m* junction
bloccato blocked; stuck
blu blue
boa *f* buoy
bocca *f* mouth
bollire boil
bollitore *m* kettle
bomba *f* bomb
borsa *f* bag
borsa dell'acqua calda *f* hot-water bottle
borsaiolo *m* pickpocket
borsellino *m* purse
borsetta *f* handbag
bosco *m* wood
bottiglia *f* bottle
bottone *m* button
braccialetto *m* bracelet
braccio *m* arm
branda *f* campbed
brandy *m* brandy
britannico British
brocca *f* jug
bruciare burn
brutto ugly
buca delle lettere *f* letterbox

bucato *m* laundry
buco *m* hole
buffo funny
buio dark
buonasera good evening
buongiorno good morning;
hello
buono good
burro *m* butter
bussola *f* compass
busta *f* envelope
butano *m* Calor gas (R)
buttare via throw away

cabina *f* cabin
cabina telefonica *f* phone
box
cacao *m* cocoa
cacciavite *m* screwdriver
cadere fall
caffè *m* coffee; **caffè
solubile** instant coffee;
caffè lungo weak black
coffee; **caffè ristretto** black
coffee stronger than
espresso
caffellatte *m* white coffee
calcio *m* football
calcolatore *m* calculator
caldo warm; hot; **fa caldo**
it's warm/ hot
caldo *m* heat
calendario *m* calendar
calmarsi calm down
calvo bald
calze *fpl* stockings
calzini *mpl* socks
calzolaio *m* cobbler
calzoncini *mpl* shorts

calzoni *mpl* trousers
cambiare change; **cambiare
treno** change trains
cambiarsi change
cambio *m* bureau de change;
gears
camera *f* room; **camera
singola/ doppia** single/
double room
camera da letto *f* bedroom
camera d'aria *f* inner tube
cameriera *f* chambermaid;
waitress
cameriere *m* waiter
camicetta *f* blouse
camicia *f* shirt
camicia da notte *f* nightdress
camion *m* lorry
camminare walk
campagna *f* countryside;
campaign
campana *f* bell
campanello *m* bell
campeggio *m* camping;
campsite
campeggio per roulotte *m*
caravan site
campo *m* field
canadese Canadian
canale *m* canal
cancello da letto gate (at airport)
candela *f* candle; spark plug
cane *m* dog
cannuccia *f* straw
canoa *f* canoe
cantare sing
canzone *f* song
capelli *mpl* hair
capire understand
capitano *m* captain
capo *m* boss
cappello *m* hat
cappotto *m* coat

capra f goat
caramella f sweet
carburatore m carburettor
carne f meat
carne macinata f minced meat
caro dear; expensive
carota f carrot
carrozza f carriage
carrozzina f pram
carta f card; paper
carta assegni f cheque card
carta da lettere f writing paper
carta da pacchi f wrapping paper
carta di credito f credit card
carta d'imbarco f boarding pass
carta igienica f toilet paper
cartella f briefcase
cartina f map
cartolina f postcard
cartone m cardboard
casa f house; **a casa** at home; **a casa di Giulia** at Giulia's; **fatto in casa** homemade
cascata f waterfall
caso m: **per caso** by chance
cassa f cash desk
cassetta f box; cassette
cassetto m drawer
castagna f chestnut
castello m castle
catena f chain
catenaccio m bolt
cattedrale f cathedral
cattivo bad
cattolico Catholic
causa f cause
cavallo m horse
cavatappi m corkscrew

caviglia f ankle
cavoletti di Bruxelles mpl Brussels sprouts
cavolfiore m cauliflower
cavolo m cabbage
c'è there is; **non c'è** he/she is not here
celibe single
cena f dinner
cenare have dinner
centigrado centigrade
centralino m operator
centro m centre
centro commerciale m shopping centre
centro della città m city centre
cercare look for
cerniera lampo f zip
cerotto m sticking plaster
certamente certainly
certificato m certificate
cestino m basket
cetriolo m cucumber
charter: volo charter m charter flight
che: la persona che the person who; **penso che** I think that; **che?** what?
chi? who?
chiamare call; **mi chiamo Marcello** my name is Marcello; **come ti chiami?** what's your name?
chiaro clear; **blu chiaro** light blue
chiave f key; spanner
chiave inglese f wrench
chiedere ask
chiesa f church
chilo m kilo
chilometro m kilometre
chiodo m nail

chitarra f guitar
chiudere close
chiudere a chiave lock
chiuso closed
ci here; there; us; each other;
  ci sono there are (see
  grammar)
ciao hello; goodbye
ciascuno each
cibo m food
ciclismo m cycling
ciclista m cyclist
cieco blind
cielo m sky
ciliegia f cherry
cima f: **in cima** at the top
cimitero m cemetery
cinema m cinema
cinghia della ventola f fan
  belt
cintura f belt
cintura di sicurezza f seat
  belt
cioccolata f chocolate;
  cioccolata al latte/ fondente
  milk/ plain chocolate;
  cioccolata calda hot
  chocolate
cipolla f onion
circa about
circonvallazione f ring road
città f town
clacson m horn
classe f class; **prima/
  seconda classe** first/ second
  class
clima m climate
coda f tail
codice della strada m
  highway code
cofano m bonnet
cogli with the (see grammar)
cognome m surname

coi with the (see grammar)
coincidenza f connection
  (travelling)
col with the (see grammar)
colazione f breakfast
colla f glue
colla with the (see grammar)
collana f necklace
collant m tights
collasso m stroke
colle with the (see grammar)
colletto m collar
collezione f collection
collina f hill
collo m neck
collo with the (see grammar)
colonna f column
colore m colour
colpa f: **è colpa mia/ sua** it's
  my/ his fault
colpire hit
colpo di sole m sunstroke
coltello m knife
come like; **bello come** as
  beautiful as; **come?**
  pardon?; how?; **come stai?**
  how are you?
cominciare begin
comitiva f group
commedia f play; comedy
commessa f shop assistant
comodo comfortable
compere fpl: **andare a fare le
  compere** go shopping
compilare fill in
compleanno m birthday;
  buon compleanno! happy
  birthday!
completamente completely;
  fully
completo full
completo m suit
complicato complicated

95

complimento *m* compliment
comporre dial
comprare buy
compreso included; **tutto compreso** all inclusive
compressa *f* tablet
con with
concerto *m* concert
concessionario *m* agent
conchiglia *f* shell
condimento per l'insalata *m* salad dressing
conferma *f*: **dare conferma** confirm
confezione *f* pack
confine *m* border
confusione *f* confusion; mess
congratulazioni! congratulations!
coniglio *m* rabbit
conoscere know
consigliare recommend
consolato *m* consulate
contagioso infectious
contante *m*: **pagare in contante** pay cash
contatto *m*: **mettersi in contatto con** contact
contento pleased
conto *m* bill
contraccettivo *m* contraceptive
contro against
controllare check
controllore *m* ticket inspector
coperchio *m* lid
coperta *f* blanket
coperto *m* cover charge; **al coperto** indoors
coraggioso brave
corda *f* rope
corpo *m* body

corrente *m* current; draught
correre run
corridoio *m* corridor
corriera *f* coach
corto short
cosa *f* thing; **cosa?** what?
coscia *f* thigh
così: così bello/ grande so beautiful/ big; **così** like this; **così così** so so
cosmetici *mpl* cosmetics
costa *f* coast
costare cost
costola *f* rib
costoletta *f* chop
costume *m* custom
costume da bagno *m* swimming costume
cotone *m* cotton
cotone idrofilo *m* cotton wool
cotto: troppo cotto overdone; **poco cotto** underdone; **ben cotto** well done
cozze *fpl* mussels
crampo *m* cramp
cravatta *f* tie
credere believe; think
crema *f* cream; custard
crema anti-insetto *f* insect repellent
crema detergente *f* cleansing cream
crema di bellezza *f* cold cream
crema doposhampoo *f* conditioner
crêpe *f* pancake
cric *m* jack
crociera *f* cruise
crostata di mele *f* apple pie
crudo raw

cruscotto *m* dashboard
cubetto di ghiaccio *m* ice cube
cuccetta *f* couchette
cucchiaio *m* spoon
cucina *f* kitchen; cooker
cucinare cook
cucire sew
cuffia da bagno *f* bathing cap
cugino *m*, cugina *f* cousin
cuocere cook; bake
cuoco *m* cook
cuoio *m* leather
cuore *m* heart
curva *f* bend
cuscino *m* pillow

D

da from; by; da quando since when; da Michela at/ to Michela's
d'accordo OK; sono d'accordo I agree
dado *m* nut
dagli, dai, dal, dalla, dalle, dallo from the; by the (*see grammar*)
danneggiare damage
dappertutto everywhere
dare give
data *f* date
dattero *m* date (*to eat*)
davanti *m* front; davanti a in front of
debole weak
decidere decide
decollare take off
degli, dei, del some; of the (*see grammar*)

delizioso lovely; delicious
della, delle, dello some; of the (*see grammar*)
deluso disappointed
dente *m* tooth
dentiera *f* dentures
dentifricio *m* toothpaste
dentista *m* dentist
dentro inside
deodorante *m* deodorant
dépliant *m* leaflet
deposito bagagli *m* left luggage
depresso depressed
destra *f* right; a destra (di) on the right (of)
detersivo liquido per i piatti *m* washing-up liquid
detersivo per bucato *m* washing powder
detestare hate
devo/ devi/ deve I/ you/ he (she) must
di of; più brutto di uglier than; tentare di fare try to do (*see grammar*)
diabetico diabetic
dialetto *m* dialect
diamante *m* diamond
diapositiva *f* slide
diario *m* diary
diarrea *f* diarrhoea
dicembre December
dieta *f* diet
dietro *m* back; dietro (a) behind
difettoso faulty
difficile difficult
dimenticare forget
dimmi? yes?
dintorni *mpl* environs; nei dintorni di in the vicinity of
di nuovo again

Dio m God
dipendere: dipende it depends
dipingere paint
dipinto m painting
dire say
diretto direct
direttore m manager
direzione f direction
disastro m disaster
disco m record
discoteca f disco
disfare: disfare le valigie unpack
disinfettante m disinfectant
disoccupato unemployed
dispiacere: le dispiace se …? do you mind if …?
dispositivo m device
distante far away
distanza f distance
distributore m distributor; dispenser; petrol station
disturbare disturb
dito m finger
dito del piede m toe
ditta f company
diverso different; **diversi** several
divertirsi have fun
dividere divide
divieto di … … forbidden
divorziato divorced
dizionario m dictionary
doccia f shower
documento m document
dogana f customs
dolce sweet
dolce m dessert
dolore m pain
doloroso painful
domanda f question
domani tomorrow

domenica Sunday
donna f woman
dopo afterwards; **dopo cena** after dinner
dopobarba m aftershave
doppio double
dormire sleep
dottore m doctor
dove where
dovere have to
droga f drug
dune fpl sand dunes
duomo m cathedral
durante during
duro hard
duty free m duty-free shop

e and
ebreo Jewish
eccetto except
ecco here is/ are; here you are; that's it
edificio m building
educato polite
elastico elastic
elastico m rubber band
elettricità f electricity
elettrico electric
elicottero m helicopter
emergenza f emergency
emorroidi fpl piles
emozionante exciting
enorme enormous
enoteca f wine tasting
entrare go in; come in
entrata f entrance
epilettico epileptic
equipaggio m crew
equitazione f horse riding

equivoco *m* misunderstanding

erba *f* grass

erbe odorose *fpl* herbs

errore *m* mistake; **per errore** by mistake

esatto correct

esaurimento nervoso *m* nervous breakdown

esempio *m* example; **per esempio** for example

esente da tasse duty-free

esposimetro *m* light meter

espresso *m* express; espresso (*coffee*); stopping train

essere be; **sono di Lucca** I come from Lucca (*see grammar*)

esso it

est *m* east

estate *f* summer

estero: all'estero abroad

estintore *m* fire extinguisher

età *f* age

etichetta *f* label

eurocheque *m* Eurocheque

Europa *f* Europe

europeo European

evitare avoid

fa ago

fabbrica *f* factory

faccia *f* face

facile easy

fagioli *mpl* beans; **fagiolini verdi** green beans

falso false

fame *f*: **ho fame** I'm hungry

famiglia *f* family

famoso famous

fare make; do; **far vedere** show

farfalla *f* butterfly

fari *mpl* headlights; **fari posteriori** rear lights

farina *f* flour

farmacia *f* chemist's

faro *m* lighthouse; light

fasciatura *f* bandage

fastidio *m* nuisance

fatica *f* strain

fattoria *f* farm

favore *m* favour; **per favore** please

fazzolettini di carta *mpl* tissues

fazzoletto *m* handkerchief

febbraio February

febbre *f* temperature; fever

febbre da fieno *f* hay fever

fegato *m* liver

felice happy

feriale: giorno feriale working day

ferita *f* wound

ferito injured

fermare stop

fermata *f* stop; **fermata dell'autobus** bus stop

fermo posta *m* poste restante

ferro *m* iron

ferro da stiro *m* iron

ferrovia *f* railway

festa *f* party; holiday

fetta *f* slice

fiammifero *m* match

fianco *m* side; hip

fidanzato engaged

fidanzato *m*, **fidanzata** *f* fiancé, fiancée

fidarsi trust

fiera *f* fair

fiero proud
figlia f daughter
figlio m son
fila f queue; **fare la fila** queue
filetto m fillet
film m film
film a colori m colour film
filo m thread
filo di ferro m wire
filtro m filter
finalmente at last
finché until
fine fine
fine f end
fine settimana m weekend
finestra f window
finire finish
fino fine; until
fioraio m florist
fiore m flower
firma f signature
firmare sign
fischio m whistle
fiume m river
flirtare flirt
foglia f leaf
föhn m hair dryer
folla f crowd
fondo m bottom; **in fondo a** at the bottom of
fondo tinta m foundation cream
fontana f fountain
footing m jogging
foratura f puncture
forbici mpl scissors
forchetta f fork
foresta f forest
forma f form; **in forma** fit
formaggio m cheese
formica f ant
fornaio m baker's

fornire supply
forno m oven
forse maybe
forte strong; loud
fortuna f luck; **buona fortuna!** good luck!
fortunatamente fortunately
foruncolo m spot
fotografare photograph
fotografia f photograph
fotografo m photographer
fra between; **fra poco** in a little while; **fra l'altro** besides other things
fragola f strawberry
francese French
Francia f France
francobollo m stamp
frasario m phrasebook
fratello m brother
frattura f fracture
freccia f indicator; arrow
freddo cold; **fa freddo** it's cold
frenare brake
freno m brake
freno a mano m handbrake
fresco fresh; cool
friggere fry
frigo m fridge
frizione f clutch; friction
frizzante fizzy
fronte f forehead; **di fronte a** opposite
frutta f fruit
frutti di mare mpl seafood
fruttivendolo m greengrocer
fucile m gun
fumare smoke
fumatori smoking (compartment)
fumo m smoke
funerale m funeral

funghi *mpl* mushrooms
funivia *f* cable car
funzionare work
fuochi d'artificio *mpl* fireworks
fuoco *m* fire
fuori outside
furgone *m* van
furioso furious
fusibile *m* fuse
futuro *m* future

G

gabbiano *m* seagull
gabinetto *m* toilet
galleria *f* tunnel
galleria d'arte *f* art gallery
gallina *f* chicken
gamba *f* leg
gambero *m* prawn
garage *m* garage
garanzia *f* guarantee
gas *m* gas
gatto *m* cat
gay gay
gelato *m* ice cream
gelo *m* frost
geloso jealous
gemelli *mpl* twins
genere *m* type; **in genere** mostly
genero *m* son-in-law
genitori *mpl* parents
gennaio January
gente *f* people
gentile kind
Germania *f* Germany
gettare throw; **gettare via** throw away
ghiaccio *m* ice

ghiacciolo *m* ice lolly
già already
giacca *f* jacket
giacca a vento *f* anorak
giallo yellow
giardino *m* garden
gin *m* gin
ginocchio *m* knee
giocare play
giocattolo *m* toy
gioco *m* game
gioielli *mpl* jewellery
gioielliere *m* jeweller's
giornalaio *m* newsagent
giornale *m* newspaper
giornata *f* day
giorno *m* day
giovane young
giovedì Thursday
giradischi *m* record player
girare turn
giro *m* turn; walk; tour; **andare in giro** walk around
gita *f* trip
gita organizzata *f* package tour
giù down
giugno June
giusto right
gli the (*see grammar*)
goccia *f* drop
gola *f* throat
golf *m* golf; jumper
gomito *m* elbow
gomma *f* rubber; tyre
gomma di scorta *f* spare tyre
gonfio swollen
gonna *f* skirt
governo *m* government
gradino *m* step
grado *m* degree
grammatica *f* grammar

Gran Bretagna f Great Britain
granchio m crab
grande big
grande magazzino m department store
grandine f hail
grasso fat
grasso m fat
gratis free
grato grateful
gratuito free
grazie thank you
grazioso pretty
Grecia f Greece
greco Greek
gridare shout
grigio grey
griglia f: **alla griglia** grilled
grosso big; thick
grotta f cave
gruccia f coathanger
gruppo m group
gruppo sanguigno m blood group
guancia f cheek
guanti mpl gloves
guardare look (at)
guardaroba m cloakroom
guasto broken; rotten
guasto m breakdown
guerra f war
guida f guide
guida telefonica f phone book
guidare guide; lead; drive
guscio m shell
gusto m taste

I

i the (see grammar)
idea f idea
idiota m idiot
idratante: prodotto idratante m moisturizer
idraulico m plumber
ieri yesterday
il the (see grammar)
imbarazzante embarrassing
imbarcarsi board
imbuto m funnel
immediatamente immediately
immersione f skin-diving
imparare learn
impermeabile m raincoat
importante important
importare: non importa it doesn't matter
impossibile impossible
imposte fpl shutters
improvvisamente suddenly
in in; into; **vado in Scozia** I am going to Scotland; **in macchina** by car
incartare wrap
incassare cash
incidente m accident
incinta pregnant
incontro m meeting
incredibile incredible
incubo m nightmare
indicare show
indietro behind; back
indigestione f indigestion
indipendente independent
indirizzo m address
industria f industry
infarto m heart attack

ITALIAN-ENGLISH

infermiera *f* nurse
infezione *f* infection
influenza *f* flu
informazione *f* information;
 **informazioni elenco
 abbonati** directory
 enquiries
Inghilterra *f* England
inglese English
inglese *m/f* Englishman/
 Englishwoman/ girl
ingoiare swallow
ingorgo *m* traffic jam
ingrandimento *m*
 enlargement
iniezione *f* injection
inizio *m* beginning
innocente innocent
inoltrare forward
inquinato polluted
insalata *f* salad
insegnante *m* teacher
insegnare teach
insetto *m* insect
insieme together
insonnia *f* insomnia
intelligente intelligent
interessante interesting
interno internal; inside;
 all'interno inside
intero whole
interruttore *m* switch
interruzione della corrente *f*
 power cut
intorno around
intossicazione alimentare *f*
 food poisoning
invalido disabled
inverno *m* winter
investire invest; knock over
invitare invite
invito *m* invitation
io I (*see grammar*)

Irlanda *f* Ireland
irlandese Irish
isola *f* island
Italia *f* Italy
italiano Italian

la the; her; it; you (*see
 grammar*)
là there; **di là** over there
labbro *m* lip
lacca per capelli *f* hair spray
lacci per le scarpe *mpl* shoe
 laces
ladro *m* thief
laggiù over there
lago *m* lake
lamentarsi complain
lametta *f* razor blade
lampada *f* lamp
lampadina *f* light bulb
lampone *m* raspberry
lana *f* wool
largo wide
lasciare leave; let
lassativo *m* laxative
lato *m* side
latte *m* milk
latte detergente *m* skin
 cleanser
latteria *f* dairy
lattina *f* can
lattuga *f* lettuce
lavabo *m* washbasin
lavanderia automatica *f*
 launderette
lavare wash; **lavare la
 biancheria** do the
 washing; **lavare i piatti** do
 the washing up

lavarsi wash
lavasecco *m* dry-cleaner's
lavatrice *f* washing machine
lavorare work
lavoro *m* work; **lavori stradali** roadworks
le the; her; you; them (*see grammar*)
lecca lecca *m* lollipop
legare tie
legge *f* law
leggere read
leggero light
legno *m* wood
lei she; her; you (*see grammar*)
lentamente slowly
lenti a contatto *fpl* contact lenses
lenti morbide *fpl* soft lenses
lenti rigide *fpl* hard lenses
lenti semi-rigide *fpl* gas permeable lenses
lento slow
lenzuolo *m* sheet
lettera *f* letter
lettino *m* cot
letto *m* bed; **un letto a una piazza/ due piazze** a single/ double bed; **letti a castello** bunk beds; **andare a letto** go to bed
leva del cambio *f* gear lever
lezione *f* lesson
li them (*see grammar*)
libbra *f* pound
libero free
libreria *f* bookshop
libretto degli assegni *m* cheque book
libro *m* book
lima per le unghie *f* nailfile
limite di velocità *m* speed limit

limonata *f* lemonade
limone *m* lemon
linea aerea *f* airline
lingua *f* tongue; language
liquore *m* liqueur; spirit
lisca *f* fishbone
liscio smooth; neat
lista *f* list; menu
lista dei vini *f* wine list
lite *f* fight
litro *m* litre
livido *m* bruise
lo the; him; it (*see grammar*)
Londra London
lontano far away
loro they; them; **il/ la loro** their; theirs (*see grammar*)
lozione solare *f* suntan lotion
luce *f* light
lucertola *f* lizard
luci di posizione *fpl* sidelights
lucido per le scarpe *m* shoe polish
luglio July
lui he; him (*see grammar*)
luna *f* moon
luna di miele *f* honeymoon
luna park *m* funfair
lunedì Monday
lunghezza *f* length
lungo long

ma but
macchia *f* stain
macchina *f* car; machine
macchina da scrivere *f* typewriter

macchina fotografica f camera

macelleria f butcher's

macho macho

madre f mother

maestro m instructor

maggio May

maggiore bigger; **la maggior parte di** most of

maglia f: **lavorare a maglia** knit

maglietta f T-shirt

maglione m sweater

mai never

maiale m pig; pork

maionese f mayonnaise

mal m: **mal di denti/ testa** toothache/ headache; **mal di gola** sore throat; **ho il mal di mare** I'm seasick

malato ill

malattia f disease

malattia venerea f VD

male badly; **far male** hurt

mamma f mum

mancare: **mi manca** I miss

mancia f tip (in restaurant etc)

mancino left-handed

mandare send

mangianastri m cassette player

mangiare eat

Manica f Channel

manica f sleeve

manifesto m poster

maniglia f handle

mano f hand; **di seconda mano** second-hand

manzo m beef

marciapiede m pavement

mare m sea; **sul mare** at the seaside

marea f tide

margarina f margarine

marito m husband

marmellata f jam; **marmellata d'arance** marmalade

marrone brown

martedì Tuesday

martello m hammer

marzo March

mascara m mascara

mascella f jaw

materasso m mattress

matita f pencil

matrimonio m wedding

mattina f morning

mattone m brick

maturo ripe

me me (see grammar)

meccanico m mechanic

medio: **di taglia media** medium-sized

medicina f medicine

medievale medieval

Medio Evo m Middle Ages

Mediterraneo m Mediterranean

medusa f jellyfish

meglio better

mela f apple

melanzana f aubergine

melone m melon

meno less

mento m chin

mentre while

menù m menu

meraviglioso wonderful

mercato m market; **a buon mercato** cheap

mercoledì Wednesday

mese m month

messa f mass

messaggio m message

mestiere m job

mestruazioni *fpl* period
metà *f* half
metallo *m* metal
metro *m* metre
metropolitana *f* underground
mettere put
mezzanotte midnight
mezza pensione *f* half board
mezzo *m* middle; **mezzo litro** half a litre
mezzogiorno midday
mezz'ora *f* half an hour
mi me; myself (*see grammar*)
mia, mie, miei my; mine (*see grammar*)
miele *m* honey
migliorare improve
migliore best
mingherlino skinny
minimo: come minimo at least
minuto *m* minute
mio my; mine (*see grammar*)
mirino *m* viewfinder
mobili *mpl* furniture
moda *f* fashion; **di moda** fashionable
moderno modern
modulo *m* form
moglie *f* wife
molla *f* spring
molletta da bucato *f* clothes peg
molo *m* quay
molto much; **molto caro** very expensive; **molto vino** a lot of wine; **molti paesi** many countries
mondo *m* world
montagna *f* mountain
monumento *m* monument
mora *f* blackberry

morbido soft
morbillo *m* measles
morire die
morso *m* bite
morte *f* death
morto dead
mosca *f* fly
mostra *f* exhibition
moto *f* motorbike
motore *m* engine
motorino *m* moped
motoscafo *m* motorboat
mucca *f* cow
multa *f* fine
municipio *m* town hall
muovere move
muro *m* wall
muscolo *m* muscle
museo *m* museum
musica *f* music
mutande *fpl* underpants; panties

nascondere hide
naso *m* nose
nastro *m* tape; ribbon
Natale *m* Christmas
nato born
natura *f* nature
naturale natural
naturalmente of course
nausea *f*: **ho la nausea** I feel sick
nave *f* ship
nazionalità *f* nationality
né ... né ... neither ... nor ...
nebbia *f* fog
necessario necessary

ITALIAN-ENGLISH

negativa *f* negative
negozio *m* shop
negozio di alimentari *m* grocer's
negli, nei, nel, nella, nelle, nello in the (*see grammar*)
nero black
nervoso nervous
nessuno no; none; nobody; nessun dubbio no doubt; da nessuna parte nowhere
neve *f* snow
nevrotico neurotic
niente nothing
night *m* night club
nipote *m* nephew
nipote *f* niece
no no; not
nocciola *f* hazelnut
noce *f* walnut
nodo *m* knot
noi we; us (*see grammar*)
noioso boring
noleggiare rent
noleggio di automobili *m* car rental
nolo *m*: a nolo for hire
nome *m* name
nome da ragazza *m* maiden name
nome di battesimo *m* Christian name
non not
nonna *f* grandmother
nonno *m* grandfather
nord *m* north
normale normal
nostra, nostre, nostri, nostro our; ours (*see grammar*)
nostalgia *f*: ho nostalgia di casa I'm homesick
notizie *fpl* news
notte *f* night; buona notte good night
novembre November
nudo naked
numero *m* number
numero di telefono *m* phone number
nuora *f* daughter-in-law
nuotare swim
nuoto *m* swimming
nuovo new; di nuovo again
nuvola *f* cloud
nuvoloso cloudy

o or; o ... o ... either ... or ...
obiettivo *m* lens; objective
oca *f* goose
occasione *f* chance; bargain
occhiali *mpl* glasses
occhiali da sole *mpl* sunglasses
occhio *m* eye
occupato engaged; busy
odiare hate
odore *m* smell
offendere offend
offrire offer
oggi today
ogni every
ognuno everyone
Olanda *f* Holland
olandese Dutch
olio *m* oil
olio d'oliva *m* olive oil
oliva *f* olive
oltre beyond; oltre a in addition to
ombra *f* shade
ombrello *m* umbrella

ombretto m eye shadow
omelette f omelette
onda f wave
onesto honest
opera f opera; **opera d'arte** work of art
operazione f operation
opuscolo m brochure
ora f hour; **che ore sono?** what time is it?
ora di punta f rush hour
orario m timetable
orchestra f orchestra
ordinare order
orecchini mpl earrings
orecchio m ear
organizzare organize
ormai by now
oro m gold
orologio m clock; watch
orribile horrible
osare dare
ospedale m hospital
ospitalità f hospitality
ospite m guest; host
osso m bone
ostello della gioventù m youth hostel
ostrica f oyster
ottenere obtain
ottico m optician
ottimista optimistic
ottimo excellent
ottobre October
otturatore m shutter
otturazione f filling
ovest m west

pacchetto m packet

pacco m package
padella f frying pan
padre m father
paesaggio m landscape
paese m country; town
pagare pay
pagina f page
paio m pair
palazzo m palace
palla f ball
pancetta f bacon
pane m bread; **pane bianco/integrale** white/ wholemeal bread
pane tostato m toast
panico m panic
panino m roll
panna f cream
panna montata f whipped cream
panne f: **restare in panne** break down
pannolino m nappy
pantaloncini da bagno mpl swimming trunks
pantaloni mpl trousers
pantofole fpl slippers
papà m dad
parabrezza m windscreen
parau·· m bumper
parcheggiare park
parcheggio m car park
parco m park
parecchi several
parecchio quite a lot
parete f wall
parlare speak
parola f word
parrucchiere m hairdresser
parte f part; **da qualche parte** somewhere; **da qualche altra parte** elsewhere; **d'altra parte**

howbeit however
partenza f departure
partire leave
partita f match (*sport*)
Pasqua f Easter
passaggio m: **dare un passaggio a** give a lift to
passaggio a livello m level crossing
passaporto m passport
passeggero m passenger
passeggiata f walk; **andare a fare una passeggiata** go for a walk
passeggino m pushchair
passo m pass; step
pasta f pasta; cake; pastry
pasticceria f cake shop
pasticcino m cake
pastiglie per la gola fpl throat pastilles
pasto m meal
patata f potato
patatine fpl crisps
patatine fritte fpl chips
patente f driving licence
pattumiera f dustbin
paura f fear; **ho paura (di)** I'm afraid (of)
pavimento m floor
pazzo mad
peccato m: **è un peccato** it's a pity
pecora f sheep
pedale m pedal
pedone m pedestrian
peggio worse
pelle f skin
pelle scamosciata f suede
pellicola f film
pene m penis
penicillina f penicillin
penna f pen

pennarello m felt-tip pen
pennello m paint brush
pennello da barba m shaving brush
pensare think
pensionato m old-age pensioner
pensione f guesthouse; **pensione completa** full board
pentola f saucepan
pepe m pepper (*spice*)
peperone m pepper (*vegetable*)
per for; by; through; in order to
pera f pear
per cento per cent
perché because; **perché?** why?
perdere lose; miss
perdita f leak
per favore please
perfetto perfect
pericolo m danger
pericoloso dangerous
periferia f suburbs
permanente f perm
permesso allowed
permesso excuse me
permesso m licence
permettere allow
però but
persino even
perso lost
persona f person
pertosse f whooping cough
pesante heavy
pesare weigh
pesca f fishing; peach
pesce m fish
pescheria f fishmonger's
peso m weight

ITALIAN-ENGLISH

pettine *m* comb
petto *m* chest
pezzi di ricambio *mpl* spare parts
pezzo *m* piece
piacere: mi piace il formaggio/ mangiare I like cheese/ eating
piacere *m* pleasure; **piacere (di conoscerla)** pleased to meet you
piacevole pleasant
piangere cry
piano *m* floor; **primo piano** first floor
piano quietly; slowly
pianta *f* plant; map
pianterreno *m* ground floor
piattino *m* saucer
piatto flat
piatto *m* plate
piazza *f* square
piccante hot (*spicy*)
piccolo small
picnic *m* picnic
piede *m* foot; **a piedi** on foot
pieno full
pietra *f* stone
pigiama *m* pyjamas
pigro lazy
pila *f* torch
pillola *f* pill
pilota *m* pilot
pinze *fpl* pliers
pinzette *fpl* tweezers
pioggia *f* rain
piovere rain; **piove** it's raining
piovra *f* octopus
pipa *f* pipe
piscina *f* swimming pool
piselli *mpl* peas

pittore *m* painter
più more; **più piccolo** smaller; **non ... più ...** no more
piuttosto rather
pizza *f* pizza
plastica *f* plastic
pneumatico *m* tyre
po' ***m*: **un po' (di) a little bit (of)
pochi: pochi turisti few tourists
pochino *m*: **un pochino** a little bit
poi then
politica *f* politics
politico political
polizia *f* police
poliziotto *m* policeman
pollame *m* poultry
pollo *m* chicken
polmoni *mpl* lungs
polmonite *f* pneumonia
polso *m* wrist
pomeriggio *m* afternoon; **alle 3 del pomeriggio** at 3 p.m.
pomodoro *m* tomato
pompelmo *m* grapefruit
ponte *m* bridge; deck
porro *m* leek
porta *f* door
portacenere *m* ashtray
portafoglio *m* wallet
portapacchi *m* roof rack
portare carry; bring
portata *f* course (*of meal*)
portauovo *m* egg cup
porte-enfant *m* carry-cot
portiere *m* porter; janitor
porto *m* harbour; port (*drink*)
porzione per bambini *f* children's portion

posate *fpl* cutlery
possibile possible
posso I can
posta *f* mail; **posta aerea** by airmail
poster *m* poster
posteriore: ruota/ sedile posteriore back wheel/ seat
postino *m* postman
posto *m* place; seat
postumi della sbornia *mpl* hangover
potere be able to
povero poor
pranzo *m* lunch
prato all'inglese *m* lawn
precedenza *f* right of way
preferire prefer
preferito favourite
prefisso *m* dialling code
pregare request
prego you're welcome; please; **prego?** pardon?
premere press
prendere take; catch; **prendere il sole** sunbathe
prenotare reserve
prenotazione *f* reservation
preoccuparsi per worry about
preparare prepare
presa *f* socket
presentare introduce
preservativo *m* condom
prestare lend
prestito *m*: **prendere a prestito** borrow
presto soon; early
prete *m* priest
previsioni del tempo *fpl* weather forecast
prezzo *m* price
prigione *f* prison

prima di before
primavera *f* spring
primo first
principale main
principe *m* prince
principessa *f* princess
principiante *m* beginner
privato private
probabilmente probably
problema *m* problem
profondo deep
profumo *m* perfume
programma *m* programme
prolunga *f* extension lead
promettere promise
pronto ready; hello (*on telephone*)
pronto soccorso *m* first aid
pronunciare pronounce
proprietario *m* owner
proprio just
prosciutto *m* ham
prossimo next
proteggere protect
proteggi-pannolino *mpl* nappy-liners
protestante Protestant
provare try; try on
prugna *f* plum
prurito *m* itch
pubblico public
pubblico *m* public; audience
pulce *f* flea
pulire clean
pulito clean
pungere sting
puntuale on time
puntura *f* bite; injection
può he/ she can
puzzo *m* stink

ITALIAN-ENGLISH

qua here; di qua over here
quadro *m* painting
qualche some
qualcosa something;
  qualcos'altro something
  else
qualcuno somebody
quale which
qualità *f* quality
quando when
quanti how many
quanto how much
quarto *m* quarter
quasi nearly
quelli, quelle those
quello, quella that; quello
  lì that (one)
questi, queste these
questo, questa this; questo
  qui this (one)
qui here

radersi shave
radio *f* radio
raffreddore *m* cold
ragazza *f* girl; girlfriend
ragazzo *m* boy; boyfriend
raggi X *mpl* X-ray
ragno *m* spider
rappresentante *m* agent
raramente seldom
raro rare
rasoio *m* razor; shaver
ratto *m* rat
re *m* king

reception *f* reception
receptionist *m/f* receptionist
reclamo *m* complaint
regalo *m* present
reggiseno *m* bra
regina *f* queen
religione *f* religion
rene *m* kidney
respirare breathe
responsabile responsible
restituire give back
resto *m* rest; change
retromarcia *f* reverse gear
reumatismo *m* rheumatism
ricco rich
ricetta *f* recipe; prescription
ricevuta *f* receipt
riconoscere recognize
ricordarsi (di) remember
ridere laugh
ridicolo ridiculous
riduttore *m* adaptor
riduzione *f* reduction
riempire fill
rifiuti *mpl* rubbish
rilassarsi relax
rimborsare refund
rimorchio *m* trailer
ringraziare thank
riparare repair
riparo *m* shelter
ripetere repeat
ripido steep
riposarsi take a rest
riscaldamento *m* heating
riscaldamento centrale *m*
  central heating
riserva *f* reserve; di riserva
  spare
riso *m* rice
rispondere answer
risposta *f* answer
ristorante *m* restaurant

ITALIAN-ENGLISH

ritardo *m* delay
rivista *f* magazine
rivoltante disgusting
roccia *f* rock
rock *m* rock music
romanzo *m* novel
rompere break
rosa pink
rosa *f* rose
rosé *m* rosé wine
rosolia *f* German measles
rossetto *m* lipstick
rosso red
rotondo round
rotto broken
roulotte *f* caravan
rovine *fpl* ruins
rubare steal
rubinetto *m* tap
rubrica *f* address book
rum *m* rum
rumore *m* noise
rumoroso noisy
ruota *f* wheel
ruscello *m* stream

sabato Saturday
sabbia *f* sand
sacchetto di plastica *m* plastic bag
sacco a pelo *m* sleeping bag
sala *f* living room
sala da pranzo *f* dining room
sala d'attesa *f* waiting room
salato savoury; salty
saldi *mpl* sale
sale *m* salt
sali da bagno *mpl* bath salts
salire go up

salmone *m* salmon
salsa *f* sauce
salsiccia *f* sausage
saltare jump
salumeria *f* delicatessen
salute *f* health; **salute!** bless you!; **alla salute!** cheers!
salvietta *f* napkin
sandali *mpl* sandals
sangue *m* blood; **al sangue** rare
sanguinare bleed
sano healthy
sapere know; **non lo so** I don't know
sapone *m* soap
sapore *m* flavour
sardina *f* sardine
sauna *f* sauna
sbagliato wrong
sbaglio *m* mistake
sbrigarsi hurry; **sbrigati!** hurry up!
scale *fpl* stairs
scampo *m* crayfish
scandaloso shocking
scapolo *m* bachelor
scarafaggio *m* cockroach
scarpe *fpl* shoes
scarpe da ginnastica *fpl* trainers
scarponi da sci *mpl* ski boots
scatola *f* box
scatola del cambio *f* gearbox
scatto *m* unit
scegliere choose
scendere go down; get off
scherzo *m* joke
schiena *f* back
schifoso foul
schiuma da barba *f* shaving foam
sci *m* ski; skiing

113

sci acquatico *m* waterski; waterskiing
sciare ski
sciarpa *f* scarf
scienza *f* science
scivolare skid
scivoloso slippery
scodella *f* bowl
scogliera *f* cliff
scomodo uncomfortable
scomparire disappear
scompartimento *m* compartment
sconto *m* discount
scontro *m* crash
scopa *f* broom
scorciatoia *f* shortcut
scorso: l'anno scorso last year
scotch *m* sellotape (*R*)
scottatura *f* burn
Scozia *f* Scotland
scozzese Scottish
scrivere write
scuola *f* school
scuro dark
scusarsi apologize; **mi scusi** sorry
se if
sebbene although
seccante annoying
secchio *m* bucket
secolo *m* century
seconda classe *f* second class
secondo *m* second
sedere *m* bottom (*of person*)
sedersi sit down
sedia *f* chair
sedia a rotelle *f* wheelchair
sedia a sdraio *f* deck chair
seggiovia *f* chairlift
segnale *m* roadsign
segreto secret
seguire follow

selvaggina *f* game
semaforo *m* traffic lights
sembrare seem
semiasse *m* axle
seminterrato *m* basement
semplice simple
sempre always
senape *f* mustard
seno *m* breast
sensato sensible
sensibile sensitive
sentiero *m* path
sentire feel; hear; smell; **mi non mi sento bene** I feel well/ unwell
senza without
separatamente separately
separato separate
sera *f* evening; **alle 11 di sera** at 11 p.m.
serata *f* evening
serbatoio *m* tank
serio serious; **sul serio** seriously; really
serpente *m* snake
serratura *f* lock
servire serve
servizio *m* service; **il prezzo del servizio** the service charge
sessista sexist
sesso *m* sex
seta *f* silk
sete *f*: **ho sete** I'm thirsty
settembre September
settimana *f* week; **due settimane** a fortnight
sfortunatamente unfortunately
sgarbato rude
sgradevole unpleasant
shock *m* shock
sì yes

ITALIAN-ENGLISH

siccome as
sicuro safe; sure
sidro *m* cider
sigaretta *f* cigarette
sigaro *m* cigar
significare mean
signora madam; Mrs; una signora a lady
signore sir; Mr; un signore a gentleman
signorina Miss
silenzio *m* silence
simile similar
simpatico nice
sinagoga *f* synagogue
sincero sincere; frank
singhiozzo *m* hiccups
sinistra *f* left; a sinistra (di) on the left (of)
siringa *f* syringe
slogare sprain
smalto per le unghie *m* nail polish
smettere stop
snello slim
so: non lo so I don't know
società *f* society; company
soffitto *m* ceiling
soggiorno *m* stay; lounge
sogno *m* dream
soldi *mpl* money
sole *m* sun
solito usual; di solito usually
solo alone; only
soluzione salina per lenti *f* soaking solution
sonnifero *m* sleeping pill
sonno *m*: ho sonno I'm sleepy
sopportare: non sopporto il formaggio I can't stand cheese

sopra above; di sopra upstairs
sopracciglio *m* eyebrow
soprannome *m* nickname
sordo deaf
sorella *f* sister
sorpassare overtake
sorpresa *f* surprise
sorridere smile
sosta vietata no parking
sotto below; di sotto downstairs
Spagna *f* Spain
spagnolo Spanish
spago *m* string
spalla *f* shoulder
spaventoso appalling
spazzola *f* brush
spazzolino da denti *m* toothbrush
specchietto retrovisore *m* rearview mirror
specchio *m* mirror
specialità *f* speciality
specialmente especially
spedire per posta post
spegnere switch off
spendere spend
sperare hope
spesa *f* shopping
spesso often
spezia *f* spice
spia *f* gauge
spiaggia *f* beach
spiccioli *mpl* change
spiegare explain
spilla *f* brooch
spilla di sicurezza *f* safety pin
spillo *m* pin
spina *f* plug; thorn
spinaci *mpl* spinach

spingere push
sponda f shore
sporco dirty
sporco maschilista m male chauvinist pig
sport m sport
sportello automatico m cash dispenser
sposato married
spuntino m snack
squadra f team
squalo m shark
stadio m stadium
stagione f season; **in alta stagione** in the high season
stagno m pond
stagnola f silver foil
stamattina this morning
stampe fpl printed matter
stampelle fpl crutches
stanco tired
stanotte tonight
stanza f room
stare stay; **sta/ non sta bene** he's well/ not well; **il blu ti sta bene** blue suits you
starter m choke
Stati Uniti mpl United States
stazione f station
stazione degli autobus f bus station
stazione di polizia f police station
stazione di servizio f petrol station
steccato m fence
stella f star
stendersi lie down
sterlina f pound (sterling)
sterzo m steering
stesso same
stirare iron
stitico constipated

stivale m boot
stivali di gomma mpl wellingtons
stoffa f material
stomaco m stomach
storia f story; history
strada f road
straniero m foreigner
straniero foreign
strano strange
stretto narrow
strillare scream
strofinaccio m tea towel
strumento musicale m musical instrument
studente m, **studentessa** f student
stufa f heater
stufo: sono stufo (di) I'm fed up (with)
stupefacente astonishing
stupido stupid
stupro m rape
su on; up
sua his; her; its; your; hers; yours (see grammar)
succedere happen
succo m juice
sud m south
sudare sweat
sue his; her; its; your; hers; yours (see grammar)
sugli, sui, sul, sulla, sulle, sullo on the (see grammar)
suo his; her; its; your; hers; yours (see grammar)
suocera f mother-in-law
suocero m father-in-law
suoi his; her; its; your; hers; yours (see grammar)
suola f sole (of shoe)
supermercato m supermarket
supplemento m supplement

ITALIAN-ENGLISH

surgelato frozen
sveglia f alarm clock
svegliare wake
svegliarsi wake up
svenire faint
sviluppare develop
svizzera f hamburger
Svizzera f Switzerland
svizzero Swiss

T

tabaccaio m tobacconist's
tabacco m tobacco
tacchino m turkey
taccuino m notebook
tachimetro m speedometer
taglia f size
tagliare cut
tagliaunghie m nail clippers
taglio m cut
taglio di capelli m haircut
talco m talcum powder
tallone m heel
tampone m tampon
tanto so much
tappeto m carpet
tappo m cap; plug; cork
tardi late
targa f number plate
tasca f pocket
tasso di cambio m exchange
  rate
tavola a vela f sailboard
tavolo m table
tazza f cup
te you (see grammar)
tè m tea
teatro m theatre
tedesco German
teiera f teapot

telefonare a ring
telefonata a carico del
  destinatario f reverse
  charge call
telefono m telephone
telegramma m telemessage
televisione f television
temperamatite m pencil
  sharpener
temperatura f temperature
temperino m penknife
tempesta f storm
tempo m time; weather
temporale m thunderstorm
tenda f curtain; tent
tenere hold; keep
tennis m tennis
tergicristallo m windscreen
  wiper
terminare end
termometro m thermometer
terra f earth
terribile terrible
teschio m skull
tessuto m material
testa f head
tetto m roof
thermos m thermos flask
ti you; yourself (see grammar)
tiepido lukewarm
timido shy
tirare pull
toccare touch; tocca a me
  this round's on me
togliere take away
toilette f toilet
tonno m tuna fish
tonsillite f tonsillitis
topo m mouse
torcia elettrica f torch
tornare come back; tornare a
  casa go home; come home
toro m bull

117

ITALIAN-ENGLISH

torre *f* tower
torta *f* cake
tosse *f* cough
tossire cough
tovaglia *f* tablecloth
tovagliolo *m* serviette
tra among
tradizionale traditional
tradizione *f* tradition
tradurre translate
traffico *m* traffic
traghetto *m* ferry
tragitto *m* route
tramonto *m* sunset
tranquillo quiet
tranne except
trapunta *f* quilt
trasmissione *f* transmission
trattoria *f* restaurant
treno *m* train
triste sad
troppo too
trovare find; **dove si trova ...?** where is ...?
trucco *m* make-up
tu you (*see grammar*)
tua your; yours (*see grammar*)
tubo *m* pipe
tubo di scappamento *m* exhaust
tue your; yours (*see grammar*)
tuffarsi dive
tuo, tuoi your; yours (*see grammar*)
tuono *m* thunder
turista *m* tourist
tuta da ginnastica *f* tracksuit
tuttavia however
tutto all; everything; **tutto il latte/ tutta la birra** all the milk/ beer; **tutti e due** both of them; **in tutto** altogether

ubriaco drunk
uccello *m* bird
uccidere kill
ufficio *m* office
ufficio ogetti smarriti *m* lost property office
ufficio postale *m* post office
uguale the same
ultimo last
umido wet
umorismo *m* humour
una a; one (*see grammar*)
unghia *f* fingernail
unguento *m* ointment
università *f* university
uno a; one (*see grammar*)
uomo *m* man
uovo *m* egg; **uovo sodo/ alla coque** hard-boiled/ boiled egg; **uova strapazzate** scrambled eggs
urgente urgent
usare use
uscire go out
uscita *f* exit; gate
uscita di sicurezza *f* emergency exit
utensili da cucina *mpl* cooking ustensils
utile useful
uva *f* grapes

vacanza *f* holiday; **vacanze estive** *fpl* summer holidays
vaccino *m* vaccination

vagina f vagina
vagone letto m sleeper
vagone ristorante m dining car
valido valid
valigia f suitcase; **fare le valigie** pack
valle f valley
valore m: **di valore** valuable
valvola f valve
vanga f spade
vaniglia f vanilla
vaporetto m steamer
varechina f bleach
variabile changeable
vasca da bagno f bathtub
vasellame m crockery
vaso m vase
vassoio m tray
vattene! go away!
vecchio old
vedere see
vedova f widow
vedovo m widower
vegetariano vegetarian
veicolo m vehicle
vela f sail; sailing
veleno m poison
veloce fast
velocemente quickly
velocità f speed
vendere sell
vendita f sale
venerdì Friday
venire come
ventilatore m fan
vento m wind
veramente really
verde green
verdura f vegetables
vero true
vescica f bladder; blister
vespa f wasp

vestaglia f dressing gown
vestire dress
vestirsi dress
vestito m dress
vetro m glass (*material*)
vi you; yourselves; each other (*see grammar*)
via f road; street
via away
viaggiare travel
viaggio m journey; **viaggio d'affari** business trip; **buon viaggio!** have a good journey!
viale m avenue
vicino a near
vicino m, **vicina** f neighbour
vietato forbidden
vigili del fuoco mpl fire brigade
vigna f vineyard
villa f villa
villaggio m village
vincere win
vino m wine; **vino rosso/ bianco/ rosé** red/ white/ rosé wine
viola purple
visita f visit
visitare visit
vista f view
visto m visa
vita f life; waist
vitamine fpl vitamins
vite f screw
vitello m veal
vivere live
vivo alive
voce f voice
voglia f: **ho voglia di** I feel like
voi you (*see grammar*)
volante m steering wheel

volare fly
volere want; **voglio** I want
   (to); **vuole ...?** do you
   want ...?; **vorrei** I would
   like (to)
volo *m* flight
volta *f* time; **una volta**
   once; **qualche volta**
   sometimes
volutamente deliberately
vomitare: sto per vomitare
   I'm going to be sick
vostra, vostre, vostri, vostro
   your; yours (*see grammar*)
vuoto empty

zaino *m* rucksack
zanzara *f* mosquito
zero zero
zia *f* aunt
zio *m* uncle
zitto quiet
zona *f* area
zona pedonale *f* pedestrian
   precinct
zoo *m* zoo
zucchero *m* sugar
zuppa *f* soup

GRAMMAR

There are two genders in Italian: masculine and feminine. The **ARTICLES** with masculine nouns, which mostly end in **-o**, are:

il, uno (the, a)	before a consonant
lo (the)	before **s** + consonant, before **z**
l', un	before a vowel

il bambino	the boy
un bambino	a boy
lo specchio	the mirror
uno specchio	a mirror
lo zingaro	the gypsy
uno zingaro	a gypsy
l'occhio	the eye
un occhio	an eye

The articles with feminine nouns, most of which end in **-a**, are:

la, una (the, a)	before a consonant
l', un'	before a vowel

la bambina	the girl
una bambina	a girl
l'albicocca	the apricot
un'albicocca	an apricot

In the **PLURAL** as a rule for nouns

-o becomes -i
-a becomes -e

and the changes for the article are:

singular	*plural*
il	i
lo, l'	gli
un, uno	dei, degli
la, l'	le
una, un'	delle

i bambini	the children
dei bambini	some children
gli specchi	the mirrors
degli specchi	some mirrors

GRAMMAR

le bambine	the girls		
delle bambine	some girls		

But there are exceptions. Here are some of the most common ones:

nouns ending in **-e** can be either *m* or *f*. There is no way to predict this. In the plural, the ending becomes **-i**.

luce	(la)	light	*pl*	luci	(le)
fiume	(il)	river	*pl*	fiumi	(i)
valle	(la)	valley	*pl*	valli	(le)
pesce	(il)	fish	*pl*	pesci	(i)

nouns which change gender in the plural:

uovo *m*	(l')	egg	*pl*	uova	(le)
dito	(il)	finger	*pl*	dita	(le)
labbro	(il)	lip	*pl*	labbra	(le)

irregular plurals:

uomo *m*	(l')	man	*pl*	uomini	(gli)
ala *f*	(l')	wing	*pl*	ali	(le)
mano	(la)	hand	*pl*	mani	(le)

Some **_PREPOSITIONS_**, when used with the article for 'the', combine to form a new word:

	il	lo	la	i	gli	le
a	al	allo	alla	ai	agli	alle
con	col	(collo)	(colla)	coi	(cogli)	(colle)
da	dal	dallo	dalla	dai	dagli	dalle
di	del	dello	della	dei	degli	delle
in	nel	nello	nella	nei	negli	nelle
su	sul	sullo	sulla	sui	sugli	sulle

andiamo allo stadio
let's go to the stadium

sono venuto a piedi dalla stazione
I walked from the station

nei bicchieri
in the glasses

sull'orlo del marciapiede
on the edge of the pavement

The forms in brackets are less common than the non-combined forms **con lo, con la, con gli** and **con le**.

GRAMMAR

The *ADJECTIVE* agrees with its noun in gender and number (singular or plural); as a rule it is positioned after the noun:

la biancheria sporca	the dirty linen
un uomo simpatico	a pleasant man
dei libri noiosi	some boring books

The *COMPARATIVE* is formed by adding **più** (more) or **meno** (less) in front of the adjective; the *SUPERLATIVE* by adding **il/la più** (the most) or **il/la meno** (the least):

le pesche sono più care delle pere
peaches are more expensive than pears

il sole è meno caldo di ieri
the sun is less warm than yesterday

questa chiesa è la più antica
this is the most ancient church

questo ristorante è il meno caro della città
this is the least expensive restaurant in town

The following common adjectives have also an irregular form of both comparative and superlative:

buono good	**migliore** better	**il migliore** the best
cattivo bad	**peggiore** worse	**il peggiore** the worst

il peggiore albergo della città
the worst hotel in town

POSSESSIVE ADJECTIVES are:

	m sing	f sing	m pl	f pl
my	il mio	la mia	i miei	le mie
your (fam)*	il tuo	la tua	i tuoi	le tue
your; his/ her	il suo	la sua	i suoi	le sue
our	il nostro	la nostra	i nostri	le nostre
your (pl)	il vostro	la vostra	i vostri	le vostre
their	il loro	la loro	i loro	le loro

* used with the **tu** form

il mio scontrino	my receipt
la mia borsetta	my handbag

When referring to family members, you drop the article:

mio fratello	my brother

Note that the **suo** form can mean either 'her' or 'his' or 'your' if you are using the polite **lei** form.

GRAMMAR

POSSESSIVE PRONOUNS, like adjectives, agree with the gender and number (singular or plural) of the noun they replace. Use the same words as for possessive adjectives:

> **prendi la tua macchina, non la nostra**
> take your car, not ours

When used after the verb 'to be' the article is dropped:

> **questo posto è mio**   this seat is mine
> **la macchina è loro**   the car is theirs

ADVERBS are formed by adding **-mente** to the feminine singular of the adjective:

lento	slow	**lentamente**	slowly

PERSONAL PRONOUNS

io	I	**me/mi**	me	**mi**	to me
tu	you	**te/ti**	you	**ti**	to you
lei	you	**lei/la**	you	**le**	to you
lui	he	**lui/lo**	him	**gli**	to him
lei	she	**lei/la**	her	**le**	to her
noi	we	**noi/ci**	us	**ci**	to us
voi	you	**voi/vi**	you	**vi**	to you
loro	they	**loro/li**	them	**loro**	to them

In Italian subject pronouns are often dropped:

> **siamo partiti ieri**   we left yesterday
> **verranno domani**   they'll come tomorrow

Subject pronouns are used to avoid confusion or to give emphasis

> **lui verrà alle tre, lei alle quattro**
> he's coming at three, she at four

> **vengo io!**
> I'm coming

There are basically two ways of saying *YOU* in Italian. For friends, relatives and children use the **tu** form. For people you don't know well use the **lei** form. The **lei** form is used with the same form of the verb as the one for 'he/she'. A plural form for both is **voi**.

Of the two optional forms given above (**me/mi** etc) the first should be used after prepositions:

> **questo è per me**   that's for me
> **dopo di lei**   after you/her

Pronouns usually come in front of the verb:

lo conosco	I know him
non ci ha veduto	he didn't see us

With *REFLEXIVE* verbs like **chiamarsi** or **alzarsi** use the following pronouns:

(with I)	**mi**	(with we)	**ci**
(with you)	**ti**	(with you)	**vi**
(with he/she/you)	**si**	(with they)	**si**

mi chiamo ...	my name is ...
come si chiama?	what's your name?
ci alziamo alle ...	we get up at ...

VERBS fall into three groups according to their endings (**-are**, **-ere**, **-ire**):

		comprare (to buy)	**credere** (to believe)	**partire** (to leave)
PRESENT TENSE				
I	**io**	compro	credo	parto
you	**tu**	compri	credi	parti
you; he/she	**lui/lei**	compra	crede	parte
we	**noi**	compriamo	crediamo	partiamo
you	**voi**	comprate	credete	partite
they	**loro**	comprano	credono	partono

PAST TENSE

io	ho comprato	ho creduto	sono partito
tu	hai comprato	hai creduto	sei partito
lui/lei	ha comprato	ha creduto	è partito
noi	abbiamo comprato	abbiamo creduto	siamo partiti
voi	avete comprato	avete creduto	siete partiti
loro	hanno comprato	hanno creduto	sono partiti

ho comprato un gelato
I (have) bought an ice cream

sono partiti ieri
they left yesterday

FUTURE TENSE (I will etc)

io	comprerò	crederò	partirò
tu	comprerai	crederai	partirai
lui/lei	comprerà	crederà	partirà
noi	compreremo	crederemo	partiremo
voi	comprerete	crederete	partirete
loro	compreranno	crederanno	partiranno

GRAMMAR

Two important irregular verbs are:

	essere (to be)		*avere* (to have)	
Present				
io	sono	I am	ho	I have
tu	sei	you are	hai	you have
lui/lei	è	he/she is; you are	ha	he/she has; you have
noi	siamo	we are	abbiamo	we have
voi	siete	you are	avete	you have
loro	sono	they are	hanno	they have

Past (had/have had; was/were/have been)

io	ho avuto	sono stato
tu	hai avuto	sei stato
lui/lei	ha avuto	è stato
noi	abbiamo avuto	siamo stati
voi	avete avuto	siete stati
loro	hanno avuto	sono stati

	fare (to do)	*bere* (to drink)	*dire* (to say)
Present			
io	faccio	bevo	dico
tu	fai	bevi	dici
lui/lei	fa	beve	dice
noi	facciamo	beviamo	diciamo
voi	fate	bevete	dite
loro	fanno	bevono	dicono

Past			
io	ho fatto	ho bevuto	ho detto
tu	hai fatto	hai bevuto	hai detto
lui/lei	ha fatto	ha bevuto	ha detto
noi	abbiamo fatto	abbiamo bevuto	abbiamo detto
vli	avete fatto	avete bevuto	avete detto
loro	hanno fatto	hanno bevuto	hanno detto

GRAMMAR

	andare	*venire*
	(to go)	(to come)
Present		
io	vado	vengo
tu	vai	vieni
lui/lei	va	viene
noi	andiamo	veniamo
voi	andate	venite
loro	vanno	vengono
Past		
io	sono andato	sono venuto
tu	sei andato	sei venuto
lui/lei	è andato	è venuto
noi	siamo andati	siamo venuti
voi	siete andati	siete venuti
loro	sono andati	sono venuti

Some other common verbs have irregular past tenses:

aprire	to open	aperto	open
chiudere	to close	chiuso	closed
mettere	to put	messo	put
morire	to die	morto	died
nascere	to be born	nato	born
potere	to be able to	potuto	have been able to
prendere	to take	preso	taken
scendere	to go down	sceso	gone down
scrivere	to write	scritto	written
vedere	to see	visto	seen

CONVERSION TABLES

metres
   1 metre = 39.37 inches or 1.09 yards

kilometres
   1 kilometre = 0.62 or approximately ⅝ mile

to convert kilometres to miles: divide by 8 and multiply by 5

kilometres:	2	3	4	5	10	100
miles:	1 .25	1 .9	2 .5	3 .1	6 .25	62 .5

miles
to convert miles to kilometres: divide by 5 and multiply by 8

miles:	1	3	5	10	20	100
kilometres:	1 .6	4 .8	8	16	32	160

kilos
   1 kilo = 2.2 or approximately 1⅕ pounds

to convert kilos to pounds: divide by 5 and multiply by 11

kilos:	4	5	10	20	30	40
pounds:	8 .8	11	22	44	66	88

pounds
   1 pound = 0.45 or approximately 5/11 kilo

litres
   1 litre = approximately 1¾ pints or 0.22 gallons

Celsius
to convert to Fahrenheit: divide by 5, multiply by 9, add 32

Celsius:	10	15	20	25	28	30	34
Fahrenheit:	50	59	68	77	82	86	93

Fahrenheit
to convert Fahrenheit to Celsius: subtract 32, multiply by 5, divide by 9